The Lord hath His way
in the whirlwind and in the storm
and the clouds are the dust of His feet.
NAHUM 1:3

"May you travel always
with the wind in your face,
and the sun on your back."
(AN ANCIENT SAYING)

Books by W. Phillip Keller

Splendor From the Sea
As a Tree Grows
Bold Under God— *A Fond Look at a Frontier Preacher*
A Shepherd Looks at Psalm 23
A Layman Looks at the Lord's Prayer
Rabboni— Which Is to Say, Master
A Shepherd Looks at the Good Shepherd and His Sheep
A Gardener Looks at the Fruits of the Spirit
Mighty Man of Valor— Gideon
Mountain Splendor
Taming Tension
Expendable
Still Waters
A Child Looks at Psalm 23
Ocean Glory
Walking With God
On Wilderness Trails
Elijah— Prophet of Power
Salt for Society
A Layman Looks at the Lamb of God
Lessons From a Sheep Dog
Wonder o' the Wind
Joshua— Mighty Warrior and Man of Faith
A Layman Looks at the Love of God
Sea Edge
David I
David II
Sky Edge: Mountaintop Meditations
Chosen Vessels
In the Master's Hands
Predators in Our Pulpits
Songs of My Soul
Thank You, Father
God Is My Delight
Strength of Soul

Wonder O' the Wind

W. Phillip Keller

kregel PUBLICATIONS

Grand Rapids, MI 49501

In gratitude to God Himself,
who,
by the Gracious wind of His Spirit
has,
in wonder, led me all my life

First paperback edition published 1993 by Kregel
Publications, a division of Kregel, Inc., P.O. Box 2607,
Grand Rapids, Michigan 49501.

Cover Photo: CLEO Freelance Photography
Cover Design: Alan G. Hartman

Library of Congress Cataloging-in-Publication Data

Keller, W. Phillip (Weldon Phillip), 1920-

Wonder O' the Wind: a common man's quest for God /
W. Phillip Keller.
    p.   cm.
  Originally published: Waco, Tex. : Word Books,
© 1982.
  1. Keller, W. Phillip (Weldon Phillips), 1920-
2. Christian biography—Canada. 3. Naturalists—
Canada—Biography. 4. Nature—Religious
aspects—Christianity. I. Title.
BR1725.K42A3   1993   209'.2—dc20   92-23988
[B]   CIP
ISBN 0-8254-2998-6 (pbk.)

2 3 4 5 6 Printing/Year 97 96 95

Printed in the United States of America

Contents

Part III. The Adventure Years

Part I

The Daydream Years

A Love for Life

THIS HAS BEEN ANOTHER one of those days when all the world pulsed with golden light. All of my being was stirred and stimulated by the vibrant life on every side. Everything I saw, sensed and shared was moved and touched by the wondrous wind of God's presence.

And I loved it all . . . all.

At dawn the rising sun spread its carpet of amber hues across the waves rolling in slow swells toward my door. Swift-winged wedges of cormorants sliced through the sunlit skies, their intense silhouettes sharp against the morning light. The song of the surf and the mating call of a mockingbird invited me to put aside pen and paper.

This I did with light heart and contented spirit. For at break of day my twenty-fifth book had just been completed.

I went to walk along the shore. I wanted time to be alone— to think leisurely thoughts, to reflect quietly on the long years granted to me in such generosity by a loving, caring, knowing God.

For I am in my sixty-second year.

And it seems that most of us are so slow of spirit, so hard of heart, so dull of discernment that we do not sense or see how wondrously the wind of God's presence has enfolded us, until we are well down the dusty road of our days. Somehow, suddenly we are startled to see that every step we took along the trail has been touched in love by our Lord.

This is the wonder of it all.

O the compassion and concern and care of our eternal companion! O the comfort, cheer and contentment of His company!

I strolled softly along the wave-washed strand of sand. The sea tides had swept them clean in the night. Not a footprint marked the beach now being brushed with brittle light.

It was a brand-new day, a brand-new beginning, another brand-new morning in a man's life. It was but one in thousands upon thousands of fresh, shining, exciting new mornings given to me in generous, joyous measure by my God.

The foaming, hissing, thundering breakers ran up across the sand. They ran back to lose themselves in the next wave. It was an endless oscillation—a powerful, pulsing motion linked to tides and currents, moon and planets, wind and weather. And I was wrapped up, too, in the wonder of it all.

In a thousand ways and in countless days, the impact of the presence of God's Spirit had likewise played upon my life. Because of it the long years had been filled with adventure, rich with excitement, replete with satisfaction.

Often, often, others had begged me to write about the wonder of it all. Perhaps this was the morning to begin, at least to make a simple start.

I found a solitary spot well beyond the end of the sandy shore. Here high, brown cliffs towered above the rocks and rubble at their base. Here the sun warmed the dun-colored clay and provided a quiet cove where a man could sit quietly and relive his love of life.

It was a morning of blue and gold and white. Blue skies, blue seas, blue islands basking in the haze on the horizon. It was also a golden spring day. Golden sunlight, golden boulders shining in the spray, golden sequins sparkling on the rolling wind-blown waves. There was whiteness, too, everywhere around me. White spray dashing over the stones, white-winged gulls crying in the wind, white shells shining in the gravel, white sails billowing in the breeze.

Wherever I turned, wherever I looked, the wind was at work. It made my whole world alive, beautiful, full of wonder. That really was the story of my whole life, wrapped in awe, joy and gratitude.

Not that there hadn't been dark days—dismal rains and stormy spells. There were, there always are, for all of us. But the beauty of it all was that through them all there persisted the presence, the power and the impact of the gentle wind of God. It was He who had shaped and made them in His own divine design.

Looking back how could one possibly retell the ten thousand touches of his life on mine? How could one recount the innumerable interludes in which life was charged with the electric excitement of new adventure? There was really no simple way, for in truth, at least seven full lives have been packed into the span of my sixty odd years.

Life for me has been an enormous adventure. It has been lived on the tiptoe of expectancy. It has been charged with stimulating enthusiasm, goodwill and good cheer . . . because God was here.

So I have decided to narrate in rather random fashion, like jewels strung on a silver thread, the high points that shine clearest in my memory. Happily the good ones far outweigh the grievous. So this story should sing with the goodness of our God.

This is a book to be read in relaxation and repose. It is made up of glimpses into a common man's travel through this world, wrapped in the awe and wonder of the Wind of God that played upon his path.

Gallant Lady

SHE WAS BRAVE! And she was beautiful!

Beautiful not only in bodily form, but also in serenity of soul, in shining of spirit.

My earliest recollections of her were of a wondrous woman of warmth, vibrancy, and overflowing good cheer. Despite the depravity and degradation of the pagan tribespeople among whom she lived and worked with such goodwill, there emanated from her an enormous enthusiasm for life.

Her hearty laughter rippled from the depths of her magnificent bosom like clear water bubbling up from a splendid mountain spring. It ran merrily around and over all who knew and loved her.

From her large, luminous, warm, brown eyes there pulsed a living light that somehow spoke of sublime inner serenity— a serenity that found its strength and stability in an intimate acquaintance with God. She knew Him, trusted Him, enjoyed Him, walked with Him as few humans ever do.

There was nothing prudish or pretentious about her.

She was too dynamic, too full of fun, too totally feminine to indulge in pretense.

Her complexion was almost flawless. Despite the dryness of the desperate African sun; despite the lack of cosmetics available to most women; despite the ravages of tropical disease—her face glowed with a radiance of remarkable joy. Her ready smile, her happy humor, her vibrant voice had

16

won her the admiration of others who often called her "Sister Sunshine."

Yet her humble home was a typical African frontier house built of crooked, hand-cut poles, plastered with mud, coated with cow dung to repel insects, and thatched with grass.

For her, life, all of life, was a great adventure with God. He and she were constant companions in an unfolding drama of divine design. Nothing that happened in her adventuresome and exciting career was ever an accident. Of this she was sure.

It mattered not whether she was planting cuttings of Golden Shower in her garden, or cleansing the ugly ulcer of a fly-ridden African, she could do it with commingled courage, love and élan.

She would tackle any task with a contagious confidence that carried her through to success. She would shake her head in glee, allowing the long, shining black locks of her lovely hair to shimmer around her in lustrous waves. "There's no such word as *can't*," she would chuckle. "Let's just do it!" And she did.

Her tiny, well-formed hands and feet were immensely strong. They had accomplished more work in her first thirty years of life than most women achieve in seventy. A certain intense determination to succeed, and succeed with distinction, marked her movements.

She was sturdy, energetic, dynamic and yet exquisitely dainty. There was a dimension of charming, captivating femininity that seldom surfaces in so many of today's mannish women. She knew she was all woman, she gloried in her charms as a special creation of winsome loveliness. Yet she never paraded her personality in pride or vanity.

A certain wondrous wholesomeness marked her life and conduct. She was born to be brave. She was bound to be beautiful. Life was for living. With joy and gracious generosity she was glad to give and give and give of herself to enrich others.

She was my mother!

Long before I appeared on the scene, her life as a young person had been a dynamic demonstration of our Father's faithfulness to one who trusted Him without flinching. In the first thirty years of her adventuresome career were packed

the power of a Living Lord who proved Himself her sole
support and strength under the most rough and rugged or-
deals.

Just yesterday I reread the brief notes she left behind telling
of those heroic years. Again, as always, they stirred my spirit
to see her emerge with such serene and shining confidence
in Christ, her beloved "Friend" and "present Companion."
How fortunate, how favored was I to have been mothered
by such a wondrous woman of incandescent faith in God.

Though she exercised that faith in beseeching God for
the well-being of her as yet unborn child; though she trusted
Him fully for my welfare all during my tender years; though
she believed implicitly that in His own good time God would
deliver me from the steel-willed waywardness of my youth,
my role in her life was fraught with agony and anguish of
heart.

This, because not until late in life was I to discover that
I could not live on the faith of my mother. It was imperative
that there be born within my own soul a simple, serene confidence in the living Christ. It was essential that my mother's
"Friend" also become my firsthand "friend." It was not
enough for me to merely be told about all the thrilling events
in which God had shown Himself so real to her.

Somehow, sometime, I had to get beyond just knowing
about my mother's God. I had to come to know Him firsthand
as my Friend—my comrade—my strength—my support in
the adventure of living.

Perhaps, I cannot be sure, the partial reason for my tardi-
ness in coming to know God in quiet trust was the overwhelming impact of such a dynamic mother. Her burning
enthusiasm for Christ, her unshakable trust in Him, her exploits overshadowed anything I ever dreamed He could do
for me.

Sometimes as she recounted the spine-chilling events of
her pioneer days I doubted indeed that God could ever dupli-
cate such exploits in my experience. So in a sense I shrank
back from setting my feet on the same tough trails she had
tramped. In a peculiar, perverse way I did not want to live
in the shadow of her gallant life for God. It is not easy to
have been borne in the womb of a woman all aglow for God
. . . as much as one might admire her later in life.

Mother grew up in a robust family of seven girls and one boy. Her father was a mighty moose of a man, who, with muscles of iron and a will tough as tungsten, hewed himself a kingdom out of the northern Canadian wilderness. With stern self-discipline he struggled to establish himself in the severe and spartan world of rock, bush and muskeg.

Where the long, cruel winters broke most men, he became a timber baron. Where the short, sultry summers with their hordes of mosquitoes and black flies dismayed others, he founded a thriving farm. Where roughness and toughness were a way of life, he and his wife raised their eight children in an atmosphere of decency and dignity.

The entire family was strong in support of the small local church. But their religion, as with so many, was largely rote and ritual. It was a mental assent to a creed without the dynamic life of God active in their affairs.

Mother was one of the first precocious children to leave the family nest. With her brilliant mind and great intelligence she finished high school at fifteen. Then she took a teaching post in a remote village at sixteen. Some of her students were big, boisterous boys older than herself. Fascinated by her unusual feminine beauty they thought they could play around with such a gorgeous girl. Quickly they learned that the kind "kid gloves" of her tenderness sheathed hands and heart of stern stuff. There was no nonsense in her one-room school house. So in short order all the students adored and respected her.

During this interval in her teenage teaching career an itinerant evangelist came to her frontier community. In forthright, fearless preaching he made clear the claims of Christ. This One, The Christ, who had come among us as a man, was none other than God, very God, in disguise, garbed in human form. He it was who in love and concern for us gave up not only His glory, but also His very life to deliver us from our dilemma. Beyond this He had triumphed over death, shattered the shackles of sin and Satan. He now lived triumphantly to set men and women free to follow Him in wondrous gratitude.

For the teenage teacher this was electrifying, challenging news. Unashamedly, enthusiastically she promptly capitulated to the call of Christ. With characteristic alacrity she determined to yield her total, life-long allegiance and un-flinching loyalty to the Lord of her life—the King of Kings. She would go anywhere, do anything, endure any hardship to serve Him who loved her so deeply.

As a mark of her complete commitment to Christ she asked to be baptized in public before her friends and students. Hearing of this, her family were horrified. They were inclined to disown her. She was even forbidden to return home.

Quickly she discovered that though it may cost nothing to come to Christ for His free forgiveness and total accep-tance, it can very well cost one *everything* to follow Him in loyal service and humble devotion.

Yet she was not a person to be dismayed by this alienation from her family. Instead she set her will to do God's will no matter the price to pay. She determined to prepare herself fully to serve anywhere on earth where her Lord might call her. There emerged in her character as a teenager this re-markable resolve ever to be at her best for God no matter how tough or trying the situation. She would flame bright amid the most drab surroundings.

With implicit, quiet, yet buoyant confidence in Christ she set off to attend Bible school in the United States. Her deep conviction was that if one was to speak for the Master and minister in His name to a broken world, it must be in the power and authority of God's own revealed Word and will. She was not a little "prima donna" parading her own captivat-ing beauty and charming personality on life's little stage. She was, rather, a humble servant prepared to lose her life in simple service to lost men and women.

In short, with all the bloom and loveliness of early woman-hood gracing her, she was ready, if necessary, to be buried in some obscure spot to reach others for God. Through the deliberate laying down of her own life she was willing to be the one the Master would use to touch thousands.

Not many teenagers are made of this stern stuff. At a period in life when most are completely preoccupied with their own personal plans and pleasure, she was totally taken up with discovering God's purposes for her.

At the Bible institute she met a young man as determined as herself to live only for the Lord. The two young zealots were drawn together irresistibly. Both felt strongly called to give themselves to Africa.

So as they saturated their spirits in the Scriptures they also basked in the blossoming beauty of a romance and courtship of divine arrangement.

Theirs was no flippant affair, so common today, of having a fling with a member of the opposite sex, hoping naively that something might just work out. Instead, these two earnest, magnificent, talented young people saw themselves drawn together within the plans of God to reach and touch and heal others at the very ends of the earth.

When, in utter earnestness, they stood hand in hand on their wedding day to take their vows of allegiance to one another there were no options left open ever to opt out of their committal. It was a case, straightforward and simple, of "until death do us part."

Little did either of them realize, as they stood together bound up in such strong love, how soon those bonds would be shattered.

Love for them would be much more than youthful daydreams, roses, candlelight, soft music and the sweet kisses and gentle caresses of the beloved. Love would also be lives laid down in total obscurity and appalling darkness to deliver others. This, too, was something of the love of God, expressed so poignantly in the poured-out life of God in Christ for His bride.

The best man who stood beside them during the wedding ceremony was an eminently successful young businessman. His name was Otto Keller.

The Agony of Africa

ONLY THOSE OF US who have lived out a segment of our lives in Africa can ever understand the depths of its pathos and pain. Despite its magnificent plains, its sweeping savannas, its mighty rain forests, its great brooding deserts lying open to the sun, it remains to this day a continent of anguish. Its people still perish under the cruel heel of the god of war. Multitudes are starved by the fury of repeated famines. Intertribal conflicts, civil war, and crushing conquest are still the warp and woof of a continent in chaos.

The New York or Los Angeles resident who lightheartedly books a flight to Nairobi or Johannesburg for fourteen days of sight-seeing in the great game parks knows nothing of the agony of Africa. For out in the bush, "out in the blue" as we used to say, there still goes on the awful struggle to survive that has ever been the legacy of this "desperate continent."

Africa to this very day still weeps and writhes beneath the blood-stained hands of atrocious oppressors. The Idi Amins and Colonel Khadafys are but the latest in a long line of tyrants to tramp underfoot their hapless victims. Slavery, superstition, and desperate degradation have always held sway in large segments of the population.

Despite announced political emancipation, despite the impact of so-called enlightened education, despite a century of Christian missions, millions of men and women are still trapped in the toils of tears and turmoil.

From the soul and spirit of this continent there ever arises to heaven the burning cry—"Come over and help us!"

My mother, as a radiant bride of twenty-one years, and her handsome young husband Karl Wittich, had heard that cry. In response to the compelling conviction of God's Spirit they responded in positive action. Stepping out in unflinching faith they sailed for East Africa with another young man, Clarence Grothaus.

Without promised support from any highly organized mission board they determined to trust only God. Not only was this for their financial affairs, but also for direct guidance in their daily deliberations. Reading through the brief résumé of those early years one is deeply moved by the implicit, childlike confidence these three young people had in their heavenly Father's care.

It was 1913 when they landed at the steaming, sultry, malaria-ridden port of Dar-es-Salaam. Here the German government officials, who then administered the territory for the Kaiser, assigned them to serve in an inland region never before touched by missionaries.

They were ecstatic with expectation. The vigor and enthusiasm of youth bound them up in this new adventure for God. Here was virgin ground in which would be sown the love of the living Christ.

Their first outpost was a disease-ridden area, inland hundreds of miles from the coast. Their initial headquarters was a crudely constructed hut of hand-hewn poles, plastered with mud and cow dung, roofed with grass thatch. To top things off the nearest water supply of any sort was nine miles away. Every drop they used had to be carried that far by one of the men.

They settled down to live among strange tribespeople, speaking a strange language. White people were as strange gods to these natives. This was a typical scenario for missionary pioneers at the turn of the century. Remarkably, both bride and groom had a unique capacity to acquire a new language and were soon able to converse with the natives.

It was decided that finding a fresh water supply was absolutely essential. So both men began to dig a well. It was a dreadful job in the tropical heat under an equatorial sun. But since the local Africans were not yet willing, or ready, for such toil, the two young Americans went to work with pick and shovel.

Finally one evening a small seep of water began to spring from the stony bottom of the well. The three young people were almost delirious with delight. They had struck water! To celebrate they drew up a kettle full and made their first pot of tea.

But there was death, not life, in that well. For some obscure reason the water was contaminated. And within three days both young men were dead. The young lady lay writhing in a delirium of agony.

When I was a small lad mother occasionally recounted the horrendous events of those days to me. With the passing now of more than half a century, many of the details have faded and been forgotten. What remains, however, is the flaming splendor of this brave young widow's faith in her heavenly Father.

There she was, half a world away from her family, her friends, her home. Alone among a strange people in a strange land, she was cut off from all human comfort and consolation. Stripped of her beloved; stripped of health; stripped of human support; she could find consolation only in Christ.

Taken by porters to a distant railway station she was deposited in a dark room, certain that she would die there. Life was cheap in the African bush. Most human bodies were tossed outside at night to be consumed by hyenas. Fortunately, she was spared that death. Instead her rugged constitution helped her to recover, and she rallied from the very verge of the grave.

Heart-broken and red-eyed with weeping, lonely and forlorn, she pled with God for release from her agony. She begged that she, too, might die. But His word to her was, "Your work in Africa is not yet done."

So with incredible courage and indomitable determination she went back to the bush—back to her humble hut of mud and thatch—back to her beloved black neighbors who now were sure she had in very truth been raised from the dead.

Almost immediately after this, the dreadful first World War

of 1914–1918 erupted like a volcano on the world scene. The deadly outfall reached as far as East Africa's bush country. There German and British troops fought fierce skirmishes across the sun-blasted countryside. Men died in bloody battles; bridges and buildings were blown into oblivion; Africans were recruited into the armed services and all communication with the outside world was cut off.

Apparently the only message ever to reach the young woman's family was a terse cable that merely stated "Karl and Clarence dead. Marion recovering!" Then a steel curtain of silence closed off all communication for the next four years.

Mother lived a spartan life at the level of her African tribespeople for the next few years. European food, much less North American fare, simply was not available. Even the most basic items such as flour, sugar, tea or coffee simply could not be found. She survived on cassava root, corn meal, bananas, and wild game. Most of her meals were cooked in clay pots over smoldering brushwood fires that burned between three stones set in the ground.

Yet amid such adversity Christ became to her the most beloved friend and intimate companion. His life, His presence, His power, and His peace gradually pervaded all of her being. Again she became a radiant, glowing witness to the wondrous wind of God's gracious Spirit who enfolded her life in His.

In a short time she became so fluent and proficient in the language of her adopted people that she was considered the leading local authority in Kiswahili. She was invited to prepare study manuals on the subject and to set the exams for anyone learning the language.

In her buoyant, beautiful way she shared the Good News of God's redeeming grace with the natives around her. Despite their shyness and reticence she won many for Christ.

Out of the laid-down lives of her two companions there began to emerge new life in those whom they had come to serve. It is always this way. In order that some may live, others must die. It is the inexorable principle which governs the earth—birth, life, death, rebirth. So out of the agony, out of the anguish, out of the awesome darkness of despair there began to blossom the new life of God in the African bush.

Beyond this there was reborn in this gallant young girl an unshakable conviction that Africa was the place of God's own special appointment for her. It was He who had brought her here; it was He who would keep and support her here; it was He who would bless her here. And it was He who in His own good time would lead her on. In such an assurance she became a formidable person of enormous faith and utter confidence in God.

Early she discovered that even though stripped of all else— still there was God. And as she often said, "When you have Him, you have everything!" Few indeed have ever really learned that lesson.

In the ebb and flow of the ferocious fighting that surged back and forth across the bush country, this beautiful young widow became an object of special intrigue to the German and British troops. From the peak of her little thatch roof she bravely flew an unusual flag. It was a homemade "Stars and Stripes" she had sewn laboriously from scraps of her own skirts. It declared bravely her total allegiance to the land of which she had become a citizen through marriage to Karl Wittich, her deceased husband.

To taunt and tease her the troops would occasionally abscond with her beloved flag as a trophy of war. Fearlessly she would pursue them through the bush and across the plains to retrieve her badge of honor. She was not one to be intimidated by the force of arms or impunity of men in uniform.

This fearless courage was to be a hallmark of her entire life. Again and again in later years I was to see her storm into native villages to rescue women and children abused and beaten by their drunken husbands and fathers. She was a lovely lady with the heart of a lion. In utter, raw, selflessness she would gladly, heroically lay down her life for the sake of others. Little marvel she became a byword of the bush. Little wonder she became "mother" to multitudes of Africans. Little surprise she was so beloved by the black people.

The dreadful, desperate war years ground on slowly. The world was bathed in blood spilled from the choicest men of the earth. In her remote encampment the young missionary was cut off from all communication abroad. She lived on quietly in stern oblivion. Her friends and family in North America knew not what had befallen her.

Finally in 1918, after five long, fierce years, she felt called of God to make her way home. The military authorities tried to dissuade her from such a dangerous mission. All the railway bridges and travel routes to the coast had either been destroyed or damaged in the fighting. The only possible route was to trek across country some 240 miles to Lake Victoria. There she might find a lake steamer to take her across to Kenya.

This she decided to do. The prospect of hiking through the bush on foot accompanied by a handful of porters was not to deter her. Much of the terrain was primitive big-game country. At night the lions and leopards would prowl around her little camp where fires burned brightly to discourage intruders.

Singing merrily in her exquisite soprano voice she maintained a high morale among the men who marched with her. And in the incredible record time of eleven days she reached the lake. It was a feat never before matched by any European.

But the blazing heat and merciless equatorial sun of the African bush had taken their toll of her strength. On board ship she collapsed into a coma from which it was assumed she would never recover.

But she reached Kisumu in Kenya. There kind frontier missionaries, hearing of her plight, took her into their homes and into their hearts. While she was convalescing, word of her arrival traveled along the underground vine of African news. A young American who was serving in Kenya's famine relief heard it. He was Otto Keller, her deceased husband's best friend. When, years before, he learned of Karl's life cut short so swiftly, he in turn had given up his brilliant career in the United States and promptly left for Africa to serve in his friend's stead.

Thus there blossomed a new romance and affection between two dedicated young people who were to become my father and my mother. Their God was not only the God of all comfort, but also of all compensation.

Breaking Barren Ground

MY FATHER, LIKE MY MOTHER, came from a humble background. His parents, too, were of rugged, self-reliant Swiss stock. They had come as early pioneers to a small rural community not far from Detroit, Michigan. There his father reared a large family of nine children, supporting them on the slim salary of a country pastor.

Dad often spoke of his own boyhood with a sense of awe and agony. So poor were conditions in that frontier home that the main diet was cottage cheese and fried potatoes; cottage cheese and fried potatoes; cottage cheese and fried potatoes. If jam ever came into the house it was such a rare delicacy one dared not put both it and butter on bread at the same time.

Despite the grim austerity and frugal life style, there emerged from that family brilliant men and women who were to make an indelible mark on their generation. Dad was one of the first to leave home. His quick mind and enormous vitality soon assured him of unique success in the building industry.

Yet, when the startling news of the early death of his two friends in East Africa reached him, he immediately decided to dedicate his life to Africa. He was determined to serve in their stead. So, setting aside all personal plans and aspirations for himself, he set sail for Mombasa in 1914.

It is a measure of the man that he was prepared to use

all his own assets to achieve this dangerous mission. He had no backing from any board. He was not supported by any society or church. He was a lone stranger, like the prophets of old, looking only to his God for guidance.

Because of the war raging between Britain and Germany, he was forced to land in Kenya. There the local government authorities promptly put him into active service for famine relief. Through this he became closely associated with Quakers who were also a force in the field. And from this there flourished a life-long companionship with "The Friends" which was to enrich his entire life. The bonds of devotion between dad and the Quaker doctor were some of the most precious I ever saw between two human beings. They were to become literal "brothers."

Very early it became apparent that my father had a remarkable gift for African languages. As he moved and worked and lived among the famished Africans, he quickly picked up the various dialects. In fact by the time he died and was buried by his beloved doctor friend, he could converse freely in five different languages.

The Africans adored him because of his ability to communicate with them so freely in their own colloquialisms. He could use their idioms to joke as they joked. He was able to speak fluently in profound parables which they understood and grasped with childlike simplicity. God, by His Spirit, had indeed given dad a special "gift of tongues" through which it could be said each man heard the Word of God in his own language.

But beyond this there was born in this young and vibrant bachelor an enormous, irresistible bond of love for the natives. In the ferocious and dreadful ordeal of the long months of famine he sat where they sat. He wept as they wept. He suffered as they suffered. He literally laid down his life that they might live. This language of love was self-evident. It forged bonds of steel that endured to the end of his days.

Few, few indeed were the foreigners who were as intensely adored and loved as dad. In later years, when as a small boy I was to accompany him on some of his treks, I could not help but marvel at the affection shown him. Men and women who may not have seen him in years would rush up to him crying out, "My father, my father," for in truth he had delivered them from death to life physically and from darkness to light spiritually.

There may have been more famous, more illustrious, more academically sophisticated scholars in the ranks of African workers, but few ever touched the heart of the Africans as he did. There flowed through the emotions, mind and will of this young man an enormous empathy for the African. He never saw himself as superior or apart from the people to whom he was called. He literally had become one with them. It was the secret of his success among them . . . to give—and give—and give, expecting nothing in return except the opportunity to please God.

Dad was a man of deep sensitivity; a man capable of entering with profound sympathy into the plight of another; one with a wide capacity to love others even though they were unlovable.

When there stood before him men who had staggered miles for a handful of meal it was as though he had walked those miles himself. When a woman came to him with a child at her breast, pulling on paps that were dry of human milk for want of food, he fought back tears from eyes that saw deeper than her black skin. When those who were stronger pushed aside thin-ribbed children in the scramble to find food for pinched stomachs, it was he who saw that the tiny ones were not trampled, shoved aside or forgotten in the crush.

No wonder they learned to love him so! No wonder that even ten, fifteen or twenty years later when he passed through their villages the people would come rushing out, crying: "Bwana Kella—Bwana Kella—our father, our father!" What obvious joy, what spontaneous delight they showed just in seeing his face again. They would grip his rough, calloused hands and cling to them feverishly—those same hands that had measured out meal, poured out water or led a little child to find its mother during those long, terrible months while famine gnashed its teeth upon their land.

Those grim days allowed no time for pious platitudes about "this or that would be in the African's best interest." Either you fed him or he dropped dead.

Here there was no room for scheming. Here there could

be no ulterior motives in which white men promoted their own ends under the guise of helping the African. Here men served their fellows and in the serving found themselves. Out of the fiery furnace there emerged friendships and loyalties that bore bonds of steel welded under the heat of an awful ordeal.

Imagine, then, what a firm foundation this was on which to launch a life's work! My father's efforts were to be undergirded with the affection of unnumbered natives. His most humble beginnings held the promise of a hundred hearts who owned him as their own. He had given and given and given of himself. One does not give without returns, as his later life proved so amply.

Finally the famine years began to wane. Rains came again to slake the thirsty ground. Springs began to flow. Tiny trickles of water ran down dry dongas, gradually gaining strength to flow full once more. New grass crept over the brown hills and carpeted the bleak plains. Maize sprouted from damp earth, its green shoots turgid with life and the promise of an abundant harvest. Shining eyes twinkled from dark faces and laughter filled the village circle again.

If there be any one reason that stands out sharply above all others for the animosity and anger shown against Europeans by Africans today, if we wish an explanation for the animallike hate that dominates national thinking throughout the continent, it can best be summed up in a sentence: "Our own failure to feel that cruel goad . . . of eternally empty stomachs."

For half a century we have been told that half the earth starves. For years beyond number the Western world has wallowed in an overabundance of food. Meanwhile millions of Chinese, Indians, and Africans, who can scarcely stay on their feet, wonder each morning if by sundown a fragment of food will have crossed their lips.

On the grain farms of North America pyramids of wheat, oats and barley have stood idle in the fields, unable to find another kernel's space in bursting, overloaded elevators. In the great fruit belts and vegetable fields hundreds upon hundreds of tons of tomatoes, potatoes, apples, oranges and peaches shrivel on the trees or rot on the land, turning back to decaying matter.

In the face of this grim imbalance our excuses for not sending more food to needy people look pathetic. Our eternal, selfish unwillingness to share with those who starve is a reflection on our democratic spirit.

Oh, yes, all the old arguments of cost of distribution; of uneconomic returns to the producers; of undermining the economy of friendly, producing nations are so often repeated they need no reiteration here.

But when governments can find funds to pay farmers actually to reduce production; when they can afford to take land out of crops to keep up prices; when they can finance untold billions for building rockets, atomic missiles and other weapons of destruction; when they can do all these with utter indifference to hungry men elsewhere, then we deserve no other fate than to be despised by a resentful Asia and Africa.

Our surplus food could have welded the strongest strands of friendship between us and underprivileged peoples. Instead it may well be the very lump on which we choke ourselves in outright gluttony.

This was the lesson learned so well in those famine years by my father . . .

To give—and give—and give.

But it was not enough to just hand out food. Behind the gesture there had to be understanding—an entering into the despair of another man's plight. Then beyond that there had to be hope—a hope that somehow tomorrow would be better and that the days ahead would find grain in the hut and grass on the hill.

It was his ambition not only to establish a mission that would minister to men's hearts but also an enterprise that would make the natives self-sufficient in their physical needs.

It was his contention that converting Africans to Christianity embraced a much wider field of earthy effort than just preaching from a pulpit. In his humble manner he loved to stand among his people under a tree, talking to them of God, rather than using a platform at all.

Fat cattle in the stalls; corn bins bulging with maize; pastures thick with grass; earth rich with glory; happy people bursting with mirth and song—this was his vision of practical Christianity in action.

He was concerned with more than just fresh thoughts and

pious principles. What about healthy bodies, wholesome huts, pure water and contented children with bright eyes and ringing laughter?

If the Africans were to enjoy these blessings, then they would have to achieve them for themselves. He was there to help them help themselves. He would set up a pilot plant—a simple demonstration on their own land to serve as a pattern which they could watch, touch, see, and feel for themselves.

It was the precise procedure used in present-day schemes such as the Canadian Colombo Plan for assistance to underprivileged countries. Only my father was twenty-five years ahead of his time!

Such fancy frills as dapper clothes, European food, higher academic niceties or mechanical contrivances beyond the reach of the native's immediate grasp had no place in his program.

Dad's feet were planted firmly on the earth. He believed unflinchingly, and lived to prove it, that if husbanded, cherished and loved, Africa's warm, wild earth would respond in splendor—the splendor of a contented people in a contented land.

The preceding pages have been lifted, in part, from my book *Splendor from the Land* written twenty years ago. It was dedicated to dad's memory and recounts in vivid detail the magnitude and impact of his life in those early days.

Soon after the famine ended, and the clouds of war were dissipated, mother and dad were married. They quickly acquired a piece of rocky land as their own. There they began the pioneer enterprise that eventually would blossom into a splendid work for God.

A year later I was born. The kindly, gentle Quaker doctor delivered me one dark night inside a simple hut built of mud and thatch that served as a humble shelter for mother and dad.

At a very early age I was fully aware that I was part of a unique multiracial family, whose arms stretched very wide. My parents, quite obviously, did not dote just on me. They were surrounded with hundreds of Africans whom they loved just as much. Their arms stretched out eagerly to embrace a large family of forlorn, helpless people on every side. I was by no means the only "star" in the galaxy of our interdependent lives.

Because the nearest white neighbors were miles away, my playmates were black boys and girls. Very readily, and rather too rapidly at times, I began to think native, act African and behave like a bushman.

With ferocious and rather formidable singleness of mind my parents literally flung themselves into the task of turning an untamed chunk of Africa into a gorgeous country estate. Sometimes, in my rather solitary moments of reflection I did wonder what mattered most to mother—her gorgeous garden, her growing girl's school, or her gamboling son.

Sometimes, in a rather melancholy mood I felt sure roses, catechism classes, and endless correspondence counted far more than my contentment. But I did not vent my feelings in rank rebellion. Instead, I simply slipped away softly to stalk wild birds or spend the sunny days in search of game animals.

At an early time in life when most youngsters are still playing with trucks and trains I was becoming a skilled and cunning hunter. I handled a sling with deadly accuracy. My pockets were worn out carrying fistfuls of small smooth stones. And I could throw a rock with such sure aim as to kill a lizard basking in the sun at a hundred feet.

At times this relentless instinct to hunt, stalk, and kill appeared to disturb dad. He, too, had become a remarkably fine marksman. The heads and hides of wild animal trophies adorned the rough walls of our home. Nor did anything stir my blood more than to listen to his hunting exploits. Yet, somehow, for some strange reason, the passion for the wild so apparent in his son made him uneasy.

Sometimes I would overhear him say to my mother, "That boy of ours seems bent on only one thing—to hunt and kill."

Little did he seem to realize that his own intense preoccupation with planting, plowing and producing crops left little time for the lad who tried to tag along behind him. Often dad gave me the distinct impression he was so deeply immersed in building churches, teaching Bible classes, holding council meetings and helping Africans, that he forgot I was even around.

Of course, this did have one dubious benefit. It gave me

the chance to raid the orchard, hunt wild mushrooms or get involved in some other mischief that often ended in a first class licking. At a very tender age I began to build high walls of self-defense around myself. With the craft and cunning of my young companions in crime I early and swiftly learned how to evade being beaten and lashed for supposed wrongdoing.

To offset all this mother taught me early to read and write. She compelled me to memorize entire chapters of Scripture. She forced me to practice the piano. She was determined to have me civilized. Yet it was only a veneer of outer education and polite adornment. I was at heart a wild, wayward, willful lad in whose veins rushed the untamed blood of an untamed land.

In truth I was an American by birth and upbringing, but an African by intimate interaction with my primitive environment.

What I did not then realize was that in truth there were forming in me two distinct personalities. One was that of a white boy who loved fine literature, good books, classical music and the proud traditions of his forebears. Sometimes in the silence of the early dawn I would dream dreams of one day making my mark in the realm of literature. I had crystal clear visions of addressing large audiences overseas in America and Canada. These came as naturally and clearly as some children dream of becoming a banker or ballerina. Yet I shared them with no one, for at that time they appeared as pure fantasy.

Now, of course, more than half a century later, I am aware they were aspirations of great promise bestowed upon me by the tender touch of my gracious and loving God. Then they were only "crystal castles" easily shattered by the stern events of a troubled youth.

The other personality impinging itself upon my malleable mind and easily molded emotions was that of a son of Africa— a product of its burning plains, blue hills and mysterious, brooding bush country. Somehow, in some strange way I was too free a spirit, too daring and adventuresome ever to be bound by walls or rules or restrictive regulations.

I was a throbbing, vital part of all things wild and free . . . the hawks that soared on rising thermals in the sun

. . . the gazelle that raced across the plain . . . the leopard that stalked the bushbuck in the night.

So I dreamed, too, of becoming a game warden, a field naturalist, an explorer, a traveler to remote places far from the clamor of civilization.

Two boys in one body. Two directions in one destiny. Two hopes throbbing in one heart. And amid all the counteracting tugs and pulls an enormous capacity for mischief.

Only God understood the tangle.

Others did not!

My mentors often regarded me, in later years, with distinct dismay. They simply assumed I was a "bad boy"—"a rather vicious individual"—with a will of steel that could only be bent and battered by ferocious beatings.

From my earliest years until my late teens I attended all sorts of schools, lived in various institutions, was subjected to life in all sorts of homes and was continually misunderstood and abused.

Ultimately only here and there did an occasional teacher or some tenderhearted homemaker take time to find the roots of my so-called rebellion.

Yet, I repeat again, my heavenly Father understood.

On the basis of His own divine disclosure in Psalm 139, I now see clearly this great truth.

First of all, only He comprehended the precise genetic structure of my person. Only He knew the fierce and determined character traits inherited from my sturdy Swiss grandparents and from my even more resolute mother and dad. All were tough, hardy, durable individuals. Only He knew the wild, free blood that not only flowed in my veins but also coursed through my brain.

Second, only God was aware of the unusual environmental impacts being made upon my life during those first tender impressionable years. Though, like so many missionary parents, my dad and mother tried to reassure me of their care, it was, at best, thinly diluted and widely divided among a thousand Africans as well.

So much of the time I felt as wind-blown as the grass on the hills . . . bent this way and that by the pressure of my African peers and playmates—as well as by the pressures of parents, teachers and hostile white schoolmates.

But also, in a special sense, in my solitary moments, I knew the presence of the wind of God's Spirit pressing on my person.

O the wonder of His touch!

Torn Up Roots

WHEN I WAS EIGHT and a half years old dad and mother decided their rambunctious boy needed the discipline of a formal education. They also felt sure it would benefit their offspring to be exposed to the company of other white children.

Because Kenya was truly frontier territory, at the end of the earth so to speak, I was obliged to be sent 250 miles away to a gaunt, gloomy edifice standing in the mist, rain, and drilling dampness of the Kenya highlands. I hated the spot from the moment I saw it.

First impressions are lasting impressions.

From that day on for the next seventeen years life for me was a stern struggle to survive in various halls and institutions of higher learning. Every hour spent within the bleak, stark walls of stone were begrudged with belligerence.

A veritable catalogue of rules, regulations, and endless restrictions imprisoned me as surely as any victim placed behind bars.

In agony of spirit and anger of emotions I would slip away to brood alone, too proud ever to show my feelings to other students or staff. Somehow I felt I had been shoved into slavery. Slavery to a school, slavery to studies, slavery to a rigid system of life that left no space for a boy to be himself.

My plight was perilously close to that of the fierce Masai.

When imprisoned for misdemeanors by the British authorities, the young warriors would simply succumb and die in their cells. Their inner spirits had been shattered. Their fierce will to live had been quenched.

And looking back in retrospect I marvel my desire to live did not die within those deadly walls.

In a trauma of terror I felt sure I had been torn loose from everything meaningful to a small lad. My home was gone. My childhood companions were gone. My beloved hills and bush of my home were gone. My dogs, my guns, my hunting escapades were gone. My long hours spent stealthily stalking things wild and challenging were gone. My drowsy hours in the sun were gone.

Now there were only gongs, bells, whistles, and teacher's barked commands regimenting every hour. Books and blackboards became the boundary of my cruel confinement. I was literally locked in an atmosphere that to my free and unshackled spirit was true torture.

Like a strip of metal heated white hot I was being pushed through a mill of terrifying intensity that twisted me into coiled spring steel.

With enormous longing I would gaze out over the wide African plains, lying warm in the sun below our forbidding forested hill. Had I felt sure I could survive long, I would have slipped away into the bush. But alone, unarmed, still but a small boy, I was sure a leopard or lion would soon have me.

This did not deter me from stealing off secretly to spend an hour or so in the dense forests around the school. This was strictly out-of-bounds. Every time I was found out, there would follow a furious licking for my foray. Sticks beyond number were broken across my back and buttocks. In fury and anger I would pick up the shattered canes and defiantly fling them at the office door.

The authorities could break their sticks on me, but they could never break my will or impose their wretched rules on me. I was born free—free as the wind off the hills.

Little did I then know that the stiff resistance, tough as tungsten, being forged in my will against all authority, would inevitably be turned as well against God. Somehow I was sure no one would ever gain control over me. No one would ever be allowed to dictate my destiny. No one would ever bind my behavior.

Fortunately for both myself and others, amid this struggle there was one person who by her quiet, strong love saved me from utter ruin. She was a tiny, hunchbacked, plain woman who taught Scripture and English in the school.

She had no idea how to dress charmingly. She used no cosmetics to cover the blemishes on her disfigured face. Her straight hair was pulled back in a simple bun. But there emanated from this gracious lady the radiant love of the living Christ that made me completely overlook any physical faults she may have had.

Through her warm, brown eyes came the compassion of one who cared deeply both for me and for God. Through her words and her actions flowed the refreshing stream of a spirit immersed in the Spirit of Christ.

She sensed my aloneness. She was aware of my fierce desire to be free. She never berated me for my behavior. Never condemned my conduct. Instead she gently came alongside to let me get a glimpse of Christ in her life. And at the same time she encouraged in me a great love of fine literature, good books, great authors.

One day, as she was speaking quietly to my parents about me, I overheard her gentle remark—"You may not believe it now, but one day God will use this lad of yours to achieve great things for His honor."

She had, unwittingly, set before me a lifelong challenge which never left me. Subconsciously I believed it could happen.

Little wonder that for more than forty years, until her death, I corresponded with her, even though we were continents apart. She was one through whom the wonder of God's wind had touched my life.

In subsequent years, whenever my far-ranging world travels took me anywhere near Great Britain, I would make time to seek out her little country cottage. There amid her roses and carnations we would sit quietly for a few moments to speak earnestly of eternal issues.

From time to time one of her unmistakable handwritten airmail letters would drop in my mail box. "What are you doing for the Master?" was her gentle question and enduring challenge. No matter how far I wandered, God, by His gracious Spirit, used the sweet influence of this gallant little lady to move upon the heartstrings of a rough, tough young man.

It would be unfair to suggest here that all my years of schooling were nothing but dismal drudgery. They, too, had their exciting moments.

In retrospect some of them are downright hilarious; others were used of Christ to impress upon me the momentous issues of life and death.

One rather boring afternoon, when a group of us thought the staff were away, we boys began a rough-and-tumble game of "Cops and Robbers." This sort of thing was ordinarily forbidden, and especially in the dark, gloomy halls of the big old building.

I had chased one lad down a long corridor. Then, hiding behind a great stone chimney in the darkness, I waited for him to return. By and by footsteps came down the hall softly. I tensed myself like a hunting leopard ready to leap on a hapless buck.

Springing out of the darkness I flung myself at the approaching victim. I wrapped my arms around my prey. To my horror I had tackled the homemaking lady and not my fellow student.

She was a big, buxom woman. Both terrified and angered by my sudden assault, she in turn threw both her ample arms around me. Then in a fit of fury she picked up my scrawny little frame and flung me hard against the wall. I was sure what few brains I had would be bashed out against the boards. Little wonder there are such irregular bumps on the back of my skull to this hour.

Today the whole scene is funny. At that moment it was serious. I would be in disgrace for months to come.

My first years at the school were complicated by my roommate. He was a boy much bigger, older and stronger than myself. He was assigned by the staff to share our very cramped quarters.

He was also a missionary kid, but a very tough one. His parents, unlike mine, had come to Africa late in life. They seemed to see in the country a unique opportunity to feather their own nests by using the Africans to serve their own ends.

This philosophy, not all that uncommon among missionaries, had rubbed off on their belligerent boy. He was a hard-headed, hard-driving, hard-living young fellow whose main aim was to make as much money as possible in trade or barter with Africans or other students at the school.

So our little room was almost like a clandestine store where he did all sorts of illicit business of which the school did not approve. He had devious and disgusting ways of operating. And because he forced me to silence it made for a very strained atmosphere. In part it simply made life in the dormitory even more grim than it might have been.

It was certainly not what it appeared to be on the surface. Fierce fights among students were common.

One very dark night, well after midnight, I was awakened by peculiar sounds of heavy panting and deep groaning from my roommate. Almost beneath his breath, but in anguish of spirit I could hear him moaning, "O God, O God, forgive me, forgive me!"

In commingled fear and daring I rose and lit my small kerosene lantern. There was no electricity at the school. Going over to his bed I saw him sitting bolt upright. In the dim lantern light I saw beads of perspiration standing out all over his forehead, face, neck and shoulders. Utter terror gripped his features.

"O God, O God!" he groaned. "I'm going to hell. I'm going to hell."

This was profound conviction, brought to bear by the powerful presence of God's Spirit in the silence and stillness of the night.

Here there were none of the superficial means used by so many preachers and evangelists to try and produce a psychological atmosphere of conviction. Here there was no soft music to try and stir a sinner's emotions. Here there was no shouting or screaming by some two-bit preacher pleading with people to repent.

Here, rather, was a soul alone, face to face with God, seeing clearly that he was undone, evil and desperately in need of mercy, pardon and forgiveness.

It was a formidable ordeal for my roommate and for me.

I opened my New Testament to the account of the terrified prisonkeeper who cried out in the middle of the night to Paul and Silas, "What must I do to be saved?" Quietly I read and reread the passage to him.

Then both of us fell to our knees by his bed. There my roommate found the forgiveness from God he sought.

It was the turning point in his life. He was in truth soundly converted. In later life he went on to become an effective evangelist for the Lord.

This deep and profound conviction of sin was an aspect of the work of God in Africa that never ceased to amaze me. Later in life, as a teenager, I was to see thousands of Africans brought to an acknowledgment of their undone condition by the Spirit of God. In their huts, in their fields, in the marketplace or in the church they would fall before God acknowledging their wrongs, confessing their sins, and seeking reconciliation.

It seldom, if ever, happens in the sophisticated society of North America. We hear much talk of "revival," but rarely see the Spirit of Christ sweep across a community in deep, life-changing conviction as in pioneer days.

Part of the reason for this is the subversive work done among us by psychologists and psychiatrists. We have been led to believe that men and women really are not sinners but rather just "sick" people. We are of the opinion that men are not really responsible for their actions. Either because of unfavorable environmental conditions or poor parenting we feel one cannot be blamed for being a crook or corrupt in character.

That night, alone with his God, my roommate knew with intense and unfeigned reality that he was a young fellow desperately in need of forgiveness for his folly.

Happily he found it. He found God to be his Father. He found Christ to be his friend. He found the gracious Spirit to be his companion, reassuring him of his total acceptance into the family of God.

It was the end of the conniving and contriving. The wheeling and dealing were over. The lying, cheating and swindling stopped. He was a remade young man. He had been torn up by the roots and replanted in Christ.

Forlorn Furlough

I WAS ALMOST ELEVEN years of age when dad and mother decided it was time for them to take a furlough. It is a remarkable measure of my father's unusual dedication to Africa that in a total of twenty-eight years of service there, he only returned to the United States twice. He sensed a keen responsibility to the young churches established by God under his leadership. Nothing was ever allowed to preempt this priority in his affairs. Kenya was his only home!

He literally laid down his life for those God had given him to love.

For reasons that still remain obscure, and very confused for me, it was felt that my parents' headquarters should be established in a peculiar little religious community in northern Illinois. They did not subscribe to the strange beliefs of the townsmen. Yet, just residing there automatically brought one into bondage to all the peculiar, self-imposed restrictions of the local populace.

It was to be my first living encounter with a so-called "cult"—an outstanding spiritual phenomenon which has always marked the religious life of the United States. And what I saw and felt and experienced in actual discrimination against myself, I came to loathe.

Like the cruel, crafty ecclesiastical hierarchy of Jesus' days on earth, so these supposedly pious prudes had insidious ways of making life miserable for common people. As our

Lord Himself said, "You bind yokes upon the people burdensome to bear."

A classic example was the absurd bylaw that in those days forbade any bus from stopping in town on Sunday. Passengers were discharged or picked up outside the town limits.

It so happened the humble little clapboard house we occupied was in the very heart of the city. One Sunday dad returned from a long tour burdened down with his huge suitcase and another heavy case containing his projection lamp and glass slides. He had no choice but to carry this tremendous load all the way home on foot.

By the time he got in the door he was one furious fellow. His anger literally flamed white hot against the pharisaical folly of supposedly superspiritual prudes. His outburst of anger helped me to fully understand the formidable imprecations made by Christ against the cultists of His day.

My memories of the year spent in that queer little community still linger on as a bad dream—a most unsettling time in my own spiritual saga. Looking back in retrospect I recognize fully now that the touch of God's gracious Spirit was playing upon my life as a young lad. But that divine wind was working in ways that I then could not fully comprehend.

There was the matter of mother's illness. She suddenly became so crippled up with acute arthritis that she could scarcely move about. Probably in part this was because of the poorly constructed little frame house we lived in. Despite our most heroic attempts to fire the old furnace, most of the heat escaped through the uninsulated walls and ceilings. It was a winter of dreadfully deep snows, and cruel icy winds swept down across the country from Canada.

Since dad was away on deputation most of the time, it fell upon me to try and maintain the house. I shoveled coal, carried out ashes and dug trails through snow drifts until winter became a formidable foe. How both mother and I longed for release and return to the gentle sunshine and warmth of a southern clime!

I had to help dress mother. I had to comb her long hair. I had to do the shopping, prepare most of our simple meals, wash the dishes and clean house—all the time watching her writhe in the excruciating agony of her crippling condition. What compounded the whole dilemma for me was that we mingled with a group of people who were forever looking for so-called "miracles." Not unlike thousands today, they were always "laying hands" on the sick. They were claiming immediate "cures." They were preaching vehemently that we are guaranteed good health as God's people.

Yet, there was mother reduced to a ghastly, deformed woman by the ravages of her rheumatoid arthritis. Nor did her condition ever moderate until once again she was able to return and live in the sunshine, warmth and comparative dryness of her African home.

So there began to arise profound questions within my own spirit as to the whole matter of physical well-being—its relationship to spiritual health. I wondered about the spurious cures claimed by so many "faith healers." The entire matter of living intelligently and harmoniously in an environment conducive to one's optimum well-being concerned me deeply.

Mother's appalling winter of wretchedness was not because of some supposed "secret sin" in her life. It was not her lack of faith. It was simply the consequence of having selected a mere "shack" of a house to live in on the shores of the wicked, wind-whipped waters of Lake Michigan.

The second great disturbing element to enter my life at this period was a certain kind of "prophetic preaching" or, as some refer to it, "end-time teaching." Like the numerous cults spawned by the unique North American culture, so this blazing, red-hot, highly charged emotional emphasis on prophecy pervaded our little community.

One can only conclude that "pickings must have been good" from the dear, gullible people of that town. Again it was my first personal encounter with so-called itinerant evangelists. Scarcely a week passed but headlines in the paper, banners across the church doors, leaflets under our front door would scream: "REVIVAL MEETINGS"—"END-TIMES PREACHING"—"PREPARE TO MEET GOD."

A certain, compelling sort of carnival atmosphere attended all of these special services. Young people in particular were literally mesmerized by them. The flaming forecasters of utter doom and sure destruction kept their audiences spell-bound with their outpourings of fire, brimstone and horrible "hells" of a dozen sorts.

These self-appointed "prophets" played upon the fears, the emotions, the ignorance of their audiences with incredible audacity. The special "spirited" music, the hair-raising anecdotes, the secret information they had on communism, socialism, dictators and political opportunists kept people in a constant ferment of anxiety and apprehension.

Many of my young associates would wend their way, often in tears and trembling, to the altar when the "invitation" was extended. What bothered me was they would go again and again. They were forever shaking in their shoes, unsure of their own salvation or the heavenly forgiveness of God.

I had never heard this particular kind of "prophetic preaching" in Africa. All of the various pastors, teachers and students of God's Word under whom I ever sat were solid men, sure of their confidence in Christ, serene and keen in their sharing the Good News with lost men and women.

Never once did I ever hear dad shout or scream in speaking to his audiences. Never did I hear him intimidate people with fearsome predictions. Never did he play upon their emotions to try and elicit a "decision."

Yet there was upon his simple preaching the profound seal of the presence of God's own Spirit. Enormous conviction came upon his hearers. So much so that by the time he died, thousands upon thousands of Africans had come to know, love and walk with Christ in beautiful communion.

So the blazing zealots who burned their way through this little town left me a bit uneasy, a bit skeptical and not a little confused about Christian teaching.

I say this in utter sincerity, simply because so many of their pyrotechnic predictions never did come to pass. Their claims proved to be false and misleading. Their exposition of Scripture was distorted. Above all they left many deluded and cynical about all things that pertained to God. Difficult doubts began to intrude themselves into my mind.

Could His Word be trusted?

Were biblical prophecies unpredictable?

Why didn't those who claimed to come to Christ go on to walk with Him in humble, happy companionship?

Statistics showed that only a small percentage of so-called "converts" under these evangelists remained true to the truth. What happened to the rest?

These, and a score of other searching, burning questions surged through my mind and emotions.

In growing stubbornness I would sit through these red-hot services, not about to buy the "big-sell." There began to build up in my young soul a distinct and dangerous distaste for all organized religion. Though only a youth I could detect the preoccupation of Christian leaders with sensationalism and "success" as measured in worldly terms.

This phenomenon still persists among many Christians. As members of our contemporary culture we are locked into the "success syndrome" of our society. We are enamored with huge campaigns, large gatherings of people, massive expenditures of money and the shattering, shaking statistics of supposed converts.

Yet everywhere I read in the Bible it impressed me that God preferred to deal with individuals in small, select encounters. Ultimately it was a man here or a woman there whose will was so totally yielded to God, they came to truly *Know Him.*

So the bombastic preaching, the sensational evangelism, the soul-stirring euphoria that engulfed me week after week only served to alienate my spirit. Now, half a century later I am thoroughly convinced that many of those who came "prophesying in the name of the Lord," claiming to do many mighty miracles in "His name," never knew Him at all nor He them (Matthew 7)!

Of course my classmates and friends were sure that my growing resentment was proof positive I was a hard-shelled sinner. My refusal to relent convinced them that this incorrigible kid from the African bush needed a heap of converting. And so in a strange sense I was discriminated against because I did not hit the sawdust trail, streaming tears of supposed remorse.

Sad to say I knew in a very deep way I was undone before my God. Rapidly I was learning how to live a very superficial, selfish life just to survive the alienation of my boyhood companions. Quickly I acquired the North American life style of living behind a false facade. Outwardly I could cunningly convince my peers that I was really "with it." Within, there raged a relentless war for my will. For whom would I live?

For God or for myself? Where were my loyalties, my true priorities in life?

Then as later, much of my spiritual solace came not from the church, but from the out-of-doors.

In the odd, rare, precious hours that I could slip away from school, and the continual chores at home, I would take to the nearby woods.

There I would follow the trails of deer and rabbits as ruthlessly as the spoor of bushbuck or leopard in Kenya. The perfect, pristine whiteness of fresh-fallen snow along a frozen stream spoke to me more profoundly about the utter purity of Christ my God, than any ranting evangelist. After all, it was He who first designed and initiated the crystalline structure of a snowflake, of which no two are ever alike. So obviously it was no problem to create people of multitudinous qualities. We were initially intended to be as pure as fresh-fallen snow, but internal decay and outward pollution soon turned the shining whiteness to gray and rotten ice.

If it happened to the whitest snow, it could also occur in the most innocuous soul of a bewildered boy.

My year of exposure to American evangelism had only served to stir up a searching, questing spirit, eager to be at peace with God, yet put off by the phony pretense of high-powered, pretentious religion.

These inner struggles were never shared with anyone.

But it was a tremendous relief when the forlorn furlough ended. With ecstatic excitement we sailed home to Kenya—to the sun and to release from false religion.

Gentle Interlude

SONGWRITERS, POETS, AUTHORS and ballad-makers have often glamorized childhood. If all of their sentiments were authentic the early years of our lives would pulse with pure delight. Growing up would be a great game. Maturing into manhood or womanhood would have a spell of magic, yes, even a touch of magnificence to it.

In a sense, only during the few, fleeting years following our furlough was this true for me. They linger rather lovingly in my memory as a gentle interlude of comparative contentment before the holocaust of high school.

Soon after our return to Kenya the gracious Spirit of God began to move, both in our home and in the African community around us, in wondrous ways. His impress on all of our lives was very real and immensely life-changing. Perhaps in my parents the impact of His presence was the most apparent.

Both dad and mother had been disillusioned by the general apathy of the church in North America. Dad in particular had traveled from coast to coast pleading with people to see the enormous need of Africa. Most of his audiences appalled him by their eagerness to hear exciting stories of the African jungle, while resisting becoming a part of the struggle to salvage and redeem a savage society.

My parents quickly concluded if God was to do a great, lasting work in His church, it would not be by human design but by the power and presence of His own sovereign Spirit bringing men and women to genuine, godly repentance. In fact, like John the Baptist of old, dad called for such a turnabout in people's lives so consistently that in typical African fashion he was called, *"Bwana Kweganira"*—which means *"Mr. Repentance."*

To his eternal credit, dad did not only teach this truth, he himself lived it out before my wondering eyes as a teenage boy. The deep changes in his own character and conduct made an enormous impact on me. With an awesome sense of respect and admiration I watched the wind of God's Spirit transform this tough, resourceful individual into a humble, tender gentleman—a prince before God and among men.

I make no claim to be an authority on revival in the church. But of one thing I am sure, no congregation, no group of lay people will ever progress any further in their walk with God than their pastor has himself gone with Christ.

It is in the pulpit that revival must start, not in the pew. Too many Christian leaders are disguised predators in the pulpit. Little wonder their people perish. See Ezekiel 34.

Not only did the wind of the Spirit work mightily in dad, but also through him, touched our entire area of the country, myself included.

What all the high-powered preaching of North America had never been able to accomplish in my stubborn will, the winsome witness of my father did. One night alone in the solitude of my own small bedroom, I came under soul-searching conviction of my own undone condition. In the clear, white, intense light of Christ's own presence I saw the appalling pride of my young, hard heart, the pollution of my own character, the rebellion of my own will.

I cried out to God for mercy, pardon and forgiveness. It was dad who in quiet strength kneeled by my side and brought me to meet the Master in contrition of spirit and deep, genuine gratitude.

This was the first of several strong links forged between my father and myself by the Spirit of God. Unlike most teenagers I did not feel any resentment against him. Rather, there grew between us bonds of mutual respect and affection. In a life style of simplicity and dignity dad walked with God as few men do.

He was not pretentious. His humor tumbled out of him

like a refreshing stream of mountain water that ran out across Africa to revitalize every life it touched. His enormous empathy with Africans gave him welcome entry into thousands of hearts and homes. He never gave the impression of a white man among blacks. He was rather a "brother," a "friend," a "father" adored and loved.

With genuine concern for my needs, he deliberately took time from enormous responsibilities of the growing church to be alone with me as I approached adolescence. Because I was away from home three-fourths of the time this was not easy. But he did his best.

It is with profound pathos that I recall our hunting trips together. He was a magnificent marksman and could handle his firearms with awesome accuracy. Patiently, thoroughly, eagerly he taught me to shoot accurately, swiftly and with deadly impact. Yet he also ingrained in me a profound respect for all life. The planet was not ours to plunder or waste. We took only the minimum to meet our most pressing needs. We preserved all we could to benefit others.

Vividly I recall one short trek we made high onto the slopes of Mount Elgon. There in the dense fragrant forests of the high country I came back one morning with a splendid trophy of a superb bushbuck. Dad's delight was as great as mine. And he took the trouble to have the hide tanned just for me.

When I was away at school he took the time to write me profound, provocative letters challenging in content, as one adult addressing another. To my dismay most of these missives were later lost in the many moves I was forced to make around the world. They were a source of wisdom, enthusiasm and sheer inspiration for one so young.

Dad simply would not settle for second best. He always insisted on several basic rules of personal behavior. "Anything worthwhile costs an effort," or "If it's worth doing, it's worth doing well," or "Opportunities only come to those prepared to grasp them," or "Do the thing you fear and so overcome."

This was strong meat for a boy attending a school where scholastic standards were a bit sloppy and social behavior was becoming increasingly permissive. Across the years the school in the highlands had come under less disciplined direction; rules were relaxed and students tended to take advantage of the more tempting freedom.

It astonished even me to see how soon some of my classmates became preoccupied with titillating friendships between opposite sexes. Somehow all the syrupy, sentimental puppy love that swirled about me seemed a bit puerile and pathetic. I for one was not much interested in being tied down by some young girl who dreamed of romance, roses and sweet kisses.

So in a strange way I became very much a loner, a lad who loved the hills, the forests, the plains, the wildlife of the bush, rather than some soft-eyed girl who sighed deeply and smiled sweetly . . . dreaming flighty daydreams.

Fortunately one of the new teachers who came to the school as I entered my teens was a remarkable woman from Boston. She was one of those rare people endowed with unusual physical beauty; hers was a magnificent mind of intense intelligence and a profound, humble love for the Lord.

She stood before us students, tall, regal, striking—like a queen in commoner's clothing. The strength of her character, the calm serenity of her gracious spirit called out the very best in me. She had been cruelly double-crossed in love. Yet it never embittered her. Rather it drove her to greater heights of undivided devotion to Christ. She was His and His alone.

So the radiance of her face was an outward reflection of her inner romance with God Himself. There moved among us one who truly was in love with Christ.

Her second great love was literature.

This she passed on to me in an exciting and stimulating introduction to some of the finest authors in the English language. She began to share with me the secrets of the power of the word written and the word spoken.

Her own diction was clear, concise and deeply moving. She conveyed to me the impression of one who "spoke as an ambassador for the King of Kings." Subconsciously I came to the conclusion that if God could make Himself so apparent in a life like hers, then possibly some day, in some way, it could happen to me.

Such is the impact of a life pure and wholesome. For this dark-haired, warm-eyed beauty with her regal bearing and gentle smile had generated within my emerging manhood not only a great fondness for fine literature, but a compelling desire to know God as she did.

Incredible as it may seem to the reader, just last Christmas, nearly fifty years later, that lady and I exchanged Christmas greetings again. Her life is still touching, enriching, uplifting mine. Through her the wind of God's Spirit played upon the deep fountains of my formative years.

The other great love that began to blossom in my boyhood was a deep-rooted love for music. My mother was endowed with a magnificent soprano voice of tremendous range and power. Whenever we attended a strange church her singing would soar above the congregation in clear, flutelike notes. Soon every head would turn to see the source of such jubilation.

For a boy this was a bit embarrassing, so I would hunch down in the pew hoping not to be noticed. But for mother just the sheer joy of singing made her oblivious to the attention she attracted.

At an early age she taught me the rudiments of piano playing. But because of my unsettled life style, shuttling back and forth to school, practice was well nigh impossible and little progress was made. But I did take up the violin. It was a portable instrument and one which could be played almost anywhere in comparative privacy.

At the school I was encouraged to pursue this musical interest. Eventually it led to a great love for classical music and the old masters. Most important, it provided a means later in life to express the profound pain and pathos which were to be a large part of my early experiences.

Often amid the loneliness, agony and heartache of faraway places the old violin would sing with sorrow and sadness no human language could ever convey.

Music for me has ever been one of the special gifts of our Father to His fragile earth children. Be it the music of waves beating out their rhythm on a beach; the melodies of wind whispering through the woods or playing upon the plain; the songs of birds and streams and happy hearts— all these cheer, lift, heal and comfort as much as Beethoven's "Moonlight Sonata" or Handel's magnificent "Messiah."

So at the school this entry into the realm of music was an introduction into a broad field of inspiration and delight that gave a new dimension to my days. For hours I would play my instrument, my audience the tall trees of the forest, letting the lucid notes flow freely out onto the wind that whipped down the hills.

The music that poured from my own hands and heart and spirit was a balm that made this fleeting, brief interlude a beautiful memory.

Another aspect of life that took on special significance for me during these early teens was the whole field of sports and athletics. Because of a quick eye, agile body, and rapid reflexes, I enjoyed such games of skill as tennis, soccer and baseball.

Both of my twin brothers had died in early infancy so there were no opportunities at home for competition with other white youngsters my age. But at the school my increasing stature and strength enabled me to gradually excel in sports. The only deterrents to becoming fully engrossed in athletics were recurring attacks of malaria, dysentery and other endemic diseases so much a part of life in Kenya in those days.

Despite these disadvantages, those few, brief, fleeting years of youthful enjoyment were satisfying and rewarding. Little did I dream that they were but a lull before the horrible hurricane about to sweep into my experience.

Hell in High School

IT WOULD BE EASIER to draw down the drapes of forgetfulness over the next four years of my life. Yet there rests upon me an obligation to relive their anguish, if for no other reason than to help other teenagers who might face such traumatic times in their experience.

The word "hell" used at the beginning of this chapter was chosen with great care. Hell in its most profound sense implies "separation from God." It carries with it that terrible torment in which a soul feels cut off from the compassion of a caring Christ.

It was suddenly decided by my parents that the sort of education offered at the mission school could not properly equip me to enter University. So I was shunted off to a tough boys' high school where there were only men teachers (so-called "masters"). There discipline was akin to that of a strict military academy. In fact the headmaster was an old British sea captain.

The first formidable shock was to be set back several years scholastically. The high academic standards of the institution were such that any "outsider" was compelled to go back and pick up all subjects never studied before. Suddenly I found myself literally buried under an overwhelming burden of books, examinations and endless hours of extra study every night.

For a wild, free, unshackled spirit like mine, this was a ghastly imprisonment. I rebelled against the restrictions of my time and energy. I was not behind bars of iron or walls of concrete—but I had been just as surely incarcerated within constricting walls of books, classes and excruciating exams.

This in itself might have been managed in due time with grim determination and stoic strength. But what began to undo me was the sudden avalanche of abuse and animosity that engulfed me from both the staff and students of the school.

Purely by accident of birth and upbringing I had been born into the home of American parents. I naturally spoke with an American accent in my speech. I tended to think, act and see life as an American does. Secondly I had been reared in a Christian home. The values, standards and commands of Christ had become an integral part of my life style.

At the Institute there was not a single godly man on the entire staff. Most of the masters were men of enormous intellectual pride, social haughtiness and intense contempt for Christians, missions, or anything to do with so-called "American religion."

In the classroom, before my classmates, these grown men, attired in their long black robes and stiff mortarboards, would berate and taunt this terrified "new boy" with the twangy American accent. Some of them were so sadistic that for the least possible excuse they would mercilessly stand me up before the other students simply to make mockery of me.

I was baited and beaten for the most minute misdemeanor. One day the mathematics master, a ferocious, red-faced, red-haired man with a bristling bronze mustache, broke a board over my buttocks with a dreadful beating just because I happened to yawn in an unguarded moment. The class of British boys found this cruel conduct highly amusing.

For me school became an appalling nightmare.

I was an innocent lad being crucified for being "different."

There are writers, journalists, reporters and countless crusaders all over the earth who speak glibly about discrimination. But unless one has actually been the victim of this horrible human behavior it is impossible to fully grasp the inner anguish of its torment and torture.

In my case, with my sensitive spirit and intense intellect, there began to be serious doubts about the genuine goodness of God. Why did He create creatures such as men capable of such cruelty? Where were justice and fairness and decency? What had I done to deserve endless abuse for no legitimate reason except the accident of birth to Christian parents? Why was I not born a Masai boy, able to grow up fully accepted, fully wanted by my fellows, free to flower into full-blown manhood as an adored warrior or junior elder?

Slowly I began to hate school and despise my British masters. I began to loathe my classmates. I began to wish I had never been born white.

My classmates were no less vindictive than their superiors. They were the sons of sophisticated, wealthy white settlers, government officials, or elite businessmen. They were arrogant young fellows who because of their British background and European culture felt a cut above anyone else. They abused the Africans, they laughed at missionaries and scorned anyone who was dumb enough to "believe" the Bible.

The upshot was that I became a prime target for some of their taunts and jeers. Wherever I went I was followed by sneers and insults. If ever tactics were designed to destroy the self-respect and self-esteem of a young person these fellows knew them. The results were traumatic for me.

I knew only intense isolation. A tight knot of inner anger like spring steel began to coil inside my consciousness.

Then one day it exploded!

I had been bullied relentlessly by a big, brawny youth who repeatedly tormented me to draw laughs from his onlooking crowd of chums. Suddenly in a fury I faced him and in low, level tones, like a lion growling its warning, I warned him: "If you touch me again, there will be trouble!"

Glibly he ignored my threat.

A growing circle of boys quickly gathered to watch him wallop me again.

In a blinding rage of commingled anger and unleashed ferociousness I leaped at him. My bare, clenched fist was aimed at his vital temple with the accuracy of a howitzer shell. It crashed against his skull. He went down as if struck by a thunderbolt of lightning.

"You've killed him, Keller! You've killed him, Keller!" the boys shouted in unison, white terror on all their tense faces.

The bully lay stretched out as a dead man. Several of the boys rushed off to bring water, but it did not revive him. Then they raced away to fetch the headmaster. He ordered the fellow to be taken to hospital.

I never spoke a single word.

In silence, alone, I walked away from the scene. From that day on no one ever dared taunt me again.

The lion had leaped! The law of the jungle had prevailed! Somehow, now, I would survive—in solitude . . . but also in deep soul-searching!

The only way I had won peace, was by war.

The very principle Jesus taught of nonviolence had been violated and produced victory.

Were the claims of Christ really valid? Did His ideas work in a wretched world of hatred, injustice and bigotry? What was a beleaguered young man to believe in? Decency or brutality?

These were searching, searing questions. Because there was no one in whom I felt I could confide, to whom I could turn in my turmoil I began seriously to question all I had been taught as a child. Was Christianity authentic in the ferocious world I lived in?

About this time both Hitler and Mussolini began to threaten, not only Europe, but all the world, with their military buildup. For years my father, who spoke perfect German, had listened to the ranting and raving of Hitler. Years before any of the politicians in Europe took the "Fuehrer" seriously, dad warned that the maniac would plunge the earth into a hellish holocaust.

But long before that the merciless Mussolini sent his minions into Abyssinia (Ethiopia) to bomb, strafe and kill the innocent villagers. Death rained down from the sky. And all of East Africa began to cringe under threat of war.

Because Kenya and Abyssinia shared a common frontier, the country was immediately put on a full military alert. An officer's training corps was set up at the school. Almost overnight the masters were strutting about in full uniform. Little did I then know some of them were hardened combat commanders from the First World War.

Before I knew what was really happening I and most of the other boys, fifteen years and over, had been issued military equipment. We each carried a .303 Lee Enfield Army rifle, a bayonet, ammunition belts and regular boots, bush hats and puttees.

Most of us lads had handled firearms for years. We could shoot with deadly accuracy and stalk our prey with cunning. We already knew all about tracking, bushcraft and the use of dead ground to outflank our quarry. In fact, we were highly skilled snipers who needed little instruction in the art of hunting or killing.

What I resented deeply was the deadly, brutal, heartless drills in hand-to-hand combat. We were taught to be steel-nerved butchers of other human beings, how to bash out a man's brains with the steel butt of the rifle, how to disembowel another with a lightning upthrust of the razor sharp bayonet, how to plunge the shining blade between his ribs to rip out his lungs or tear open his heart.

For a lad still only in his teens this was stern stuff. We were not playing war games on some puny computer screen. We were locked into the deadly game of real death and grim survival. This became even more obvious when we did field maneuvers equipped with gas masks and all the other reminders that in the war, sure to come, some of us would be slaughtered in bloody battles.

All of this was terribly sobering. My late teen years were not taken up with asking dad if I could have the car to take out some sweet young girl on a romantic date. They were taken up with wondering if there would be any future at all.

Alone, in my solitary moments, I began to doubt whether God was really around or even cared. In an ominous, horrendous, helpless way I began to think God was abandoning the world as it plunged headlong into a hell of bombings, brutality and utter human bestiality.

My spiritual searchings and solemn heart-quests for truth and veracity amid the mounting mayhem were further complicated by a strange twist of events.

About this time it became compulsory for us boys to sit under the tutelage of a so-called "chaplain." Whether or not this was to prepare us for the rôle of army chaplains in combat, remains unclear.

What I do know now is that it was my first exposure to the devastating destructiveness of so-called "higher criticism" in Christian teaching. Already I had endured fierce assaults at the school on my physical body; I had been subjected to cruel attacks on my moral fiber and self-esteem as a person; now came the outright charge against my spiritual life and faith in God and His Word.

In smooth, subtle and suggestive ways the chaplain deprecated the deity of Christ. He cast ribald ridicule on Christ's redemptive death and resurrection. He made the miracles to be but the figment of men's imaginations. The historical Old Testament narrative was held up to scholastic scorn as a compilation of unreliable folk tales. So in short the foundations upon which my boyhood faith had been built were blasted, shaken and cracked by the incredible cunning of this chaplain who claimed to speak for God.

I was falling prey to another predator in the pulpit.

Increasingly it seemed Christ was becoming ever more remote—more unreal—more unreachable.

Yet in a tender, touching way, His Spirit still swept into my awareness during the hours of dawn when I would slip outside softly to take a stroll on the dew-spangled grass.

His consolation to me was—"You will survive! You do have a future in My plans for you! This hell, too, will pass!"

First proof of this was my final graduation from that grim institution with first-class honors.

The African Awakening

THOUGH THE YEARS in high school were like a dark and ominous cloud of foreboding, they did possess a silver lining. That lining was the stirring, wondrous work of the wind of God's Spirit at work in the African community at home.

At school, more than 300 miles from home, it may have seemed in my lonely struggles of spirit that God had almost gone out of my life. Of course now, looking back in retrospect, I am keenly aware He was always there. But in the profound subjective struggles of my soul then, I often felt destitute, forlorn and forsaken.

But when I returned home for the brief weeks of holiday it was to see a whole new world in which God was very active, very alive, very real. And it would be a distinct disservice in this narrative not to tell a little of the mighty impact those events made, not only on my own life, but also in the life of the African church.

Dad and mother were people of unusual foresight. It was a special spiritual gift they both possessed for the work of the Lord. Dad, in particular, was perhaps twenty-five years ahead of his time. He always, ever envisioned an African church which would be self-governing, self-supporting and self-perpetuating. He was completely opposed to the common concept, then in vogue, that massive amounts of money, hundreds of white personnel, and endless supplies of sophisticated European technology should be poured into the missionary enterprise.

He was also strongly averse to the idea of imposing Western culture and Western civilization (so-called) upon the African—especially if this was to be equated with Christianity.

Surely it had been seen, the world over, how easy it was to produce "rice Christians" in Asia or "kaffir corn Christians" in Africa.

If a solid church was to be established in the African culture it would have to be both spiritually sound and socially stable. It was not a case, as so many contend, of either evangelism or social service, but rather a question of combining both in a total ministry to the whole man.

So it was that my parents came to the African with outstretched, open hands. In the one they bore the Good News of the gospel of Christ—the forgiveness of God, Christ's acceptance of His followers into His family. In the other hand they brought better crops, finer livestock, improved hygiene, medical aid, new schools and building trades all designed to build an improved society.

Dad often declared vehemently, "You simply cannot have contented African Christians with eternally empty stomachs." He knew full well that if a church was to thrive and counter the onslaughts of evil in a pagan society both the spiritual and physical hunger of the people had to be met.

So great was his vision, so broad his outlook, that he had little patience with the petty white missionaries who came to the country claiming they had only been called to preach or teach or do some special single service.

When Jesus the Master was here among us He engaged in every sort of activity in order to minister to all men in need. He preached. He taught. He healed. He counseled. He fed the hungry. He labored as a carpenter. He played with children. He fished. He traveled. He went about doing good in an outpouring of total selflessness.

Who, then, are men to go pirouetting through life on the slim and slippery pretext that they have just been called to some single, special ministry?

So it was that both my father and mother literally poured

their lives out for and to the people of their adoption. They simply gave and gave and gave of all they owned, whether money, time, energy, intelligence, skills or unabashed love and compassion. There simply was no holding back.

They preached; they prayed; they plowed ground; they planted the seed of God's Word; they planted fruits, vegetables, trees and grass imported from abroad. God saw all of it and was pleased to bless in a mighty abundance.

I would come home on holidays awestruck by the great things taking place—not only in a physical dimension around our home but also in a spiritual explosion within the African community.

Dad had taught the natives to master such skills as making brick, sawing lumber, stonemasonry, common carpentry, improved livestock husbandry, contour farming, special crop selection, water conservation and healthier eating habits.

He delighted just as much in seeing their fields flourish as he did in seeing the prolific production of the fruits of the Spirit in their personal relationships. As far as he was concerned God was as much the Lord of the harvest in a crop of converts as in a crop of corn. And he looked for bountiful yields in both.

Africans would walk miles to come and see the gigantic stalks and huge ears of corn that flourished in our fields. They would go home with a handful of seed to plant in their own stony fields. They also came miles to hear the Word of God, and went home with a heartful of this new precious "seed" in their stony souls.

To me, a growing lad, a maturing young man, the sheer dynamic and magnificent momentum of the whole mission was awesome. If, at school, books and exams and masters and military service and the dry discourses of the "dead" chaplain left me disillusioned, here at home there was tremendous spiritual stimulation.

Through the living love of my parents I acquired an enormous fondness for the soil, for plants, trees, shrubs, flowers, crops and grass. I came to love all livestock: fine cattle, quality breeding stock, dogs and other domesticated animals. And I also came to love the Africans with profound empathy and deep understanding. Their open transparency, their happy humor, their lilting laughter, their sweet singing, their sincere spiritual life left an indelible mark upon me.

At dawn, or just before, I would slip out of the house softly to go in search of game. I took delight in providing our table with roasted wild Guinea fowl, or duiker or bushbuck steaks. These were a delicacy and diversion from the tough African beef.

But more important than my hunting was the sound I could hear of Mooga praying in his hut, located about a block from our house. Mooga was an old man when he finally capitulated to Christ. He was too far advanced in years ever to learn to read or write. So his children read the Scriptures to him as they sat by their smoky brushwood fire in the center of his hut.

This little man took God's Word personally, very directly to his own heart. In simple, implicit response to it he prayed persistently, day and night for a great work of redemption to be done among his pagan people. God's Spirit heard those heart cries as clearly as I did when I went out at daybreak with gun in hand.

The ultimate result was a remarkable awakening among the Africans. I have deliberately declined to use the word "revival"—this because it generally implies the reviving of that which was formerly alive, but has become dead or almost deceased. This was not the case in our community.

From the very beginning of their work dad and mother had seen a steady though rather slow growth in the church. They longed for God to touch and transform more of the tribespeople. In fact, without shame or apology they pled with tears for their people to repent. They, too, prayed earnestly for the darkened society in which they labored with such love.

To their eternal credit, neither of them ever took honor to themselves for the great things God would eventually do. Instead, I often heard them remark that it was Mooga's intercession that had prevailed with God's Spirit.

For, when, in due time, The Wind of God's divine Spirit swept through the countryside, quite literally thousands of Africans were awakened from their spiritual sleep to face the white light of God's presence among them. It was in truth and in fact a visitation from above. Men and women knew they were sinners. They knew they were at odds with God. They knew they had wronged their families, their friends, their neighbors.

Convincing, life-changing, habit-breaking conviction gripped the minds, emotions and wills of people. In their huts, in their fields, in the market places, on the foot paths, in the little churches scattered across the country, men and women cried out to God for mercy. They came running to Christ. They found forgiveness for their wrongs. They found freedom from their guilt. They found themselves born anew into the family of their Father God.

Those were stirring times.

They did not leave me untouched, though my experiences at school had begun to build a tough crust of reserve around me. In a sense I felt myself to be more of an observer, a bystander, an onlooker watching The Wind of God's Spirit at work in the world.

Despite all the deprecations heaped upon Christ by the chaplain, here before my wondering eyes I saw living, irrefutable evidence of the power and presence of the living Lord. Still, strange as it may sound, absurd as it may seem, like the cynics in Jesus' own day, the miracles did not move me to greater belief in Him.

This is but one example of how a person may know all about Christ—in an objective manner—yet not really "know Him" in a dynamic inner dimension of subjective reality.

Still, I was surprised, stimulated and impressed by the powerful progress of my parents' endeavors for God and His people. Outlying churches began to spring up all over the countryside. Buildings were erected with amazing rapidity. Classes were conducted to instruct teachers, lay leaders and earnest young pastors. Their numbers seemed to increase and multiply by geometric progression. Huge services were held for those seeking church membership and instruction. Baptismal events were overwhelming with hundreds coming down to the streams for this sacrament.

The last Christmas I was home, it was decided to have three separate conventions in three different centers. At each of these well over ten thousand Africans gathered for praise and prayer in the shade of the tall Eucalyptus trees. The services lasted for hours. Anyone with spiritual perception knew God was among His people, in power and splendor.

Amid all of these exciting events, dad was kind enough not to forget or overlook my needs as a maturing teenager. During the few random hours we could share, he challenged me with increasing responsibilities in running the crews of laborers in his employ. Early in life he had taught me the great dignity of work well done. He showed me by his own shining example that success in any endeavor was 90 percent diligent hard labor and 10 percent inspiration or genius.

He often remarked, "The world is full of dreamy-eyed idealists who won't lift a finger to make their dreams come to life!"

He was intensely concerned about my own ambitions and aspirations. He cared profoundly about my deep desire to become a field naturalist, a wildlife specialist or professional resource conservationist. Yet opportunities for training in such fields were rare in those days. Any university offering courses in these scientific disciplines charged astronomical fees far beyond our frugal finances.

Dad and I would occasionally sit on the cattle corrals at sundown watching the sleek, contented beasts chewing their cuds. There our conversation would ramble over the possible alternatives my future training might take. It was man-to-man talk.

Finally we concluded that a thorough grounding in land management, animal husbandry, soil conservation and crop production would be a sound basis on which to build other careers. The University of Toronto, with its world famous, highly respected College of Agriculture at Guelph, Ontario, Canada, offered outstanding courses in these disciplines.

Most important, it provided employment to overseas students, like myself, who were obliged to work their way as best they could.

So the die was cast. Canada was where I would go to be trained as a scientist. It was far away and all a bit scary.

Heading North

SOMEHOW MY FATHER seemed to have a pronounced premonition that when we parted the next time, it would also be for the last time on earth. Though he was barely fifty years of age he held the conviction that his call "home" was not far distant.

If ever a man lived ready to die, it was he. There were no old grudges, outstanding grievances or unpaid accounts in his relationships with others. Like the meticulous set of books he kept in his business, so his life conduct was clear, clean and free of any encumbrances.

In his humble, quiet, humorous way he tried to prepare me for the perils and pitfalls of a rough-and-tumble world. War clouds, black with danger and freighted with foreboding of the fury about to engulf the earth, loomed ever larger on the horizon of our little lives.

In concern and deep affection for me he accompanied me all the way to the hot, steamy, sultry port of Mombasa, 600 miles from home. There I would board a British ship that would bear me away, never to be seen again. It was not an easy parting. It was not just a father and son who stood on the deck under a fierce equatorial sun saying farewell. It was two fond friends.

His very last words to me were never to be forgotten: "Son, when a man's ways please the Lord, he maketh even his enemies to be at peace with him" (Prov. 16:7).

Little did I realize then how desperately I would need that advice for the rest of my days. Little did I know how deeply I would grieve God in the years ahead. Little did dad know of the diabolical dangers I would face in a world where I would feel utterly unwanted and unknown . . . where a young man begins to become very tough and rough, yes, even reprobate.

The ship pulled away from the hot Kenya coast, and as evening descended the last faint blue smudge of land faded on the horizon. A sensation of intense pathos engulfed me. The pain of parting from the land of my birth and boyhood was excruciating. Had I not feared the fierce sharks of the Indian Ocean, I would seriously have considered diving overboard and swimming back to shore.

Three days later Hitler's Panzer Divisions thundered into Poland. Britain declared war on Germany, and the world went mad. Our ship was in the Suez Canal. Along with forty other merchantmen we were promptly formed into the first official convoy of the war. Accompanied by destroyers, cruisers and aircraft from the British naval base at Alexandria, we left for London.

My booking had been for New York via Genoa, Italy. That was all forgotten. Caught up in the weird web of war, I was given no choice in travel plans. Britain it had to be. Now all that mattered was surviving the stealthy attacks of submarines that skulked below the surface of the shining blue Mediterranean, and grim, gray Atlantic.

On board, life became a microcosm of human society. Most sea voyages only take a few days. We were to be incarcerated on this old steamer more than ten weeks. Any convoy travels at the speed of its slowest tramps. In some of the great autumn gales we encountered later in the Bay of Biscay we only made three nautical miles in twenty-four hours of heavy steaming.

Passengers on board began to drop their masks of respectability. The raw, gross side of human behavior began to emerge from behind the thin cosmetics of so-called civilized sophistication.

Blatantly, openly, unashamedly, several striking French women, with wanton eyes and flickering eyelashes, plied their prostitution among the passengers.

It so happened one of my former violin teachers was on board, taking his frail wife out of the tropics, back to the cool climate of the British Isles. To my utter dismay and anger he abandoned her on board to take up with a tempting young thing he found to be more fun. It shook my confidence in human conduct and commitment. How could a (supposedly) civilized man be so cruel, so uncaring?

His pale-faced, gaunt, frail little wife literally died by degrees, slumped in her deck chair by the rail. She was to be buried at sea, broken in heart, shattered in spirit, before we set eyes on the white cliffs of Dover.

Several young men, a few years older than myself, had befriended me at first. They seemed to sense my intense loneliness. But as the weeks moved on in monotonous boredom it became obvious they were indulging in homosexual activities. And when they propositioned me to participate I was both frightened and furious. Their smooth, sweet talk, their subtle insinuations, their beguiling behavior literally made my blood run cold. From deep within me there arose a deep loathing for their lusting. Being "gay" is a sordid old game.

Even among the sailors and seamen there began to be an open degeneracy. The officers seemed to delight in trying to seduce as many of the female passengers as possible. They were to be seen slinking about the ship like predators on the prowl.

What the seamen lacked in glamor they more than made up for with lurid language and ribald stories.

So amid the mayhem of a world at war, we were a shipload of people given over to animal passions and beastly behavior of barbaric proportions.

From then on I never held much respect for the so-called sophistication of Western society or the veneer of its sordid culture. Insofar as I could ascertain, it was every bit as gross, every bit as contemptible as any pagan, savage society whose members ran around naked or draped in animal skins.

What I had discovered so dramatically of the degeneracy of our much-vaunted "white" Western society, thousands of Africans were to find in the armed forces. They were recruited in droves, sent off to the fighting fronts in Burma, Ethiopia and the Middle East. What they learned in the agony of a white man's war was that Europeans and Americans were not "little white gods," but similar human beings subject to all the same traits of sin, evil and violence as themselves.

Little marvel that when the battle thunder ended, and the roaring rifles fell silent, the cry that went up from the colonies was, *"Uhuru!"*—FREEDOM! Give us freedom!

Having reached Britain, I wondered what to do. One way and another our convoy had survived the submarines and the diving Stuka bombers. I tried to find a ship to take me back to Kenya, but no passage was available. So in desperation I boarded a North Atlantic tramp and pushed on to Canada, certain the college would never admit me so late in the academic year.

The ocean crossing was a terror. Time and time again in the shrieking storms that sent thunderous gray waves crashing over our bows, I was sure we would founder. So, too, were the salty old seamen who claimed it was the worst crossing they ever endured.

Most of my time was at the rail or in the filthy washroom trying to throw up with awful *mal-de-mer*. It was impossible to keep any food down. Rapidly I lost condition, so when at last I set foot ashore I was like a walking skeleton. In all, since sailing from Mombasa I had lost forty pounds in weight.

But perhaps much more dangerously I had lost my respect and esteem for the decency and dignity of humanity. A deadly drift into despising my race had set into my soul.

I came to the college with a defiant chip on my shoulder, sure that here again I would be the "odd man out" because of my African background. If I was even admitted, I was prepared to fight for my rights. If necessary I would knock down anyone who dared to insult me or cast any reflection in my face.

To my astonishment the registrar said that I could enroll, having come so far under such difficulties. But unless I met the institute's high standards by year's end I could not stay.

Much to my surprise the average age of my fellow freshmen was 28. These were mostly "Depression youths" who had worked for years and years saving up what few dollars they could to attend the classes and take the heavy four-year courses. Even more astonishing was the openhearted generosity with which they extended their comradeship to me as a latecomer. I did not have to fight for respect or recognition in establishing myself.

What did begin to trouble me was the growing awareness that though I had come to a so-called Christian country, I was actually living among very pagan people. In my entire freshman year I found only two other students who were Christians—one the son of missionary parents in Angola, the other a quiet Mennonite youth from a farm in Southern Ontario.

I joined the only active, regular, student Christian club on campus and was taken aback to find fewer than a dozen Christians attended. Even more astonishing was the discovery that out of the entire staff of over 136 professors, only one dared to fearlessly take his stand as Christ's person.

In reality, I was in a highly respected institution of so-called higher learning, from which God had been effectively excluded. His name was never mentioned there, except in profanity. And anyone holding Christian views was regarded with humiliating disdain as rather "dull."

The campus itself, reputed to be one of the most beautiful in all of North America, sat perched on a high rise of land referred to as "The Hill." Its broad rolling acres (more than 1500 of them) were meticulously groomed and cared for by a huge staff. For this was also Ontario's leading experimental station in crops, livestock, fruit, poultry and horticulture. It was not only a magnificent collection of fields, orchards, barns, greenhouses and laboratories, but also an impressive research center.

At the foot of the "Hill," in the nearby town, I found a small, struggling church, to which I could walk easily. Because it was so handy, it became my spiritual home. Had I been able to afford bus fare, I might have gone further in search of a more stable congregation. But money was so scarce my lot seemed to be cast with this lame little place and its peculiar pastor.

If nothing else, attending this place of worship gave me a clear insight into the dreadful deadness of ten thousand other similar struggling churches scattered across the country. The pastor, an ex-carpenter, should have long since gone back to his hammer and nails, instead of "hammering" his people Sunday after Sunday. He would rant and rave and roar with stentorious voice and clenched fist. At times I was tempted to walk out in sheer disgust.

Strange as it seems now, it was sitting in that cold, drafty, bleak clapboard church I promised God that if ever I was given opportunity to speak for Him, I would never scream or holler at His people. Even in those far-off, grim, northern days the warm wind of Christ's Spirit convinced me that there were better ways to turn men to Himself than through empty, hollow tirades. Shouting was no substitute for proper preparation of soul and spirit before God.

During the full four years I studied on the hill, I seldom neglected to attend the little church. It was a peculiar phenomenon. For steadily, persistently, under the impact of evolutionary studies in all the fields of my discipline my faith in God's Word was being eroded away. This was true both in scientific dimension as well as the philosophical approach to life.

Few Christians in our society seem to be aware that the evolutionary hypothesis, if pursued to its logical conclusion, insists philosophically that man, not God Himself, is the ultimate being in the universe. It concludes that since man is the end product of pure chance, mere accident, he need not be responsible or answerable to any higher authority. This, of course, is the main creed of humanism.

This all being the case, one must conclude, if he is not a Christian, that every individual is free to believe as he wishes, do as he likes, without respect or regard for any higher frame of reference or standard of conduct.

Are we appalled at the rampant revolutionary forces at work in the world that have emerged from this idea? All the systems, ideologies and false propaganda promulgated on the planet since the days of Darwin have had this as their seedbed.

I became an ardent, keen, impressionable scientific student. I was not immune to the subtle insinuations implanted in my mind during the long lectures and intense laboratory sessions. All of them were set in a direction opposite to what the minister preached from his pathetic little pulpit. I was being torn in two.

It was not difficult to catch up on my studies. I could readily grasp the courses. In fact at the end of the first year I stood sixth with distinction. But within my spirit a further definite drift from God had begun. Dark doubts had been cast upon the Scriptures. I began to wonder in Canada if Christianity was credible.

The one bright exception to the spiritual gloom during this difficult time was the lovingkindness of a dear couple in a nearby town. Often on weekends they would invite me to their home. What a joyous relief from the heavy, steady schedule at college!

The lady was my cousin, a gorgeous woman who carried herself like a queen with a shining, radiant spirit. Her husband was an eminently successful businessman in the community who encouraged me much in my career.

In their gentle, quiet way they provided a touch of tenderness to life, which otherwise would have been totally lacking from those rugged years. I was deeply grateful for their affection and generous hospitality.

Part II

The Rugged Years

The Farm

ONE OF THE STRINGENT requirements of the University in those days was that every student had to have practical field experience in his discipline. It was not enough just to know the theories or attend the lectures. One had to live on the land, become familiar firsthand with crops, livestock and weather. He had to "know" the basic resources of the ecosystem.

Consequently I was compelled to find employment on a farm. I hoped the owner would pay enough in wages to enable me to work my way through the courses during the coming year. This would be augmented by work after classes, with some assistance from my parents' mission society.

Because of my unfamiliarity with northern farming practices it was not easy to find anyone who would take me on. As with most young people I was up against the age-old problem—"Employers want experienced help, but how do you get experience if no one will hire you?" A vicious trap to break out of.

To my unbounded relief a grizzled, frontier farmer in northern Ontario decided to take a chance on this kid from Kenya. He really did not risk much, for his offer was to give me room and board, plus the princely sum of $1.00 per day for wages.

What he did not tell me when I agreed to work for him for five months, was that "my day" would begin at 5:00 A.M.

and end whenever it became dark. In northern Ontario in mid-June it is not dark until 11:00 P.M.!

The vivid experiences of that traumatic time will never leave me. I have recounted them at length elsewhere. The exciting episodes in the sugar bush, the handling of horses, the runaway team, the lonely dog, the flaming fall interludes—all are told there.

But this book is not about the land. It is about the tremendous inner spiritual struggles in the stony soil of my soul.

For as a young man, I found the farm almost my total undoing in terms of my walk with Christ. In quiet, gentle earnestness, I shall endeavor to recount those days as objectively as possible without undue prejudice or adverse reflection on anyone involved.

Before I do so, perhaps it will help the reader to understand just a little of the biblical background against which these events took place. Then I shall not be charged with undue bias or bigotry.

It must ever be said to my mother's credit that she saturated my soul in the Scriptures. By the age of six I had memorized whole sections of God's Word from both the Old and New Testaments. So, during the subsequent years of my life, no matter where I went or how far from God my footsteps strayed, the gracious Spirit of God had used His own Word as a bridgehead to my innermost spirit. Through the memorized passages God could minister to me as a man. He was faithful to do that, always!

By the time I was twenty, and went to the farm, I had been taught by teachers and preachers drawn from a wide spectrum of Protestantism. My own parents were deeply influenced by the Keswick emphasis on the deeper life in Christ. Dad had encouraged me to read many Keswick messages. Some of my parents' dearest friends were Quakers. Often the two couples shared their beliefs. Dad held enormous respect for outstanding great and godly men in the Church of England. At school my mentors had been Methodists, Baptists or devout Presbyterians.

Later, in high school my "homes away from home" had been among Salvation Army enthusiasts or stern Brethren people. I had sat under the ministry of the most conservative Church of Scotland men and also the most liberal modernists of the Army chaplaincy.

So, in a sense, I should have been more or less "shock-proof" to whatever new teaching came along. I really was not—possibly because it was so closely and intensely intertwined with the events of my daily work on the farm.

My employer was a sinewy, strong, raw-boned man who never stopped babbling about the Bible. From the very first, awful day in which we spent almost ten hours shoveling a nauseating mountain of manure from the dark pit behind his barn, he assailed me with his interpretation of prophecy. He was an elder in his local church and took pride in his pastor's frequent visits to the farm.

The church, to which he insisted on taking me, was an extreme group of charismatic people, who were much given to ecstatic emotionalism. The services with their shouting, their spectacular outbursts of praise, their utterances in unknown tongues, and their dramatic displays of feeling made me uneasy.

The distinct impression that came to my spirit was that these dear people were simply getting "high" on emotional excitement—that they were far less concerned with "The Most High!" And to compound the confusion they claimed a certain sort of superspirituality that the rest of us common mortals lacked.

The aged farmer in particular was a point in case. He would rise to his feet in the services and with arms raised toward the rafters, sway from side to side as he spoke in a torrent of unintelligible sounds. This was said to be a special outpouring of divine disclosures given to him from above.

Yet out on the farm he behaved harshly in his abuse of man and beast who worked for him.

Even his faithful collie, who cringed from his presence, slinking away in fear at his approach, felt the fury of his anger.

In the milking barn he would berate his patient cows confined in their grim, cold, narrow stalls. Again and again I saw him strike them over the back with the manure fork. The poor things had no room to run, no place to hide from his temper.

When his own grown sons came home the odd weekend, the visit would almost invariably erupt into a family feud. So fierce were the accusations and counter accusations hurled against each other, I simply could not bear to be about the house. So I would slip out the door, away into the fields, just to find release from the heat of the arguments.

This same elder never ceased to taunt me about my own beliefs. He and his fellow church leaders seemed convinced I was not a "convert." They were certain I needed to be reformed. And they were determined to do something about it. All of which may have been well intentioned.

Along with other reluctant recruits I would be escorted down into the so-called "tarrying-meetings" in the basement of the church. A group would gather round, shouting, gesticulating, laying hands on me to receive the "baptism."

In a twisted, tormented way I was being turned against the church—or at least against this style of superficial spirituality. Nor was the archenemy of my soul slack in exploiting the doubts and disparagement that were emerging within my spirit against Christianity.

It was a precarious period in my walk with God. I was so dismayed that I found little inclination to even pray or seek the solace of God's Spirit. If anything it seemed I had come under the influence of false spirits in the sensational services to which I was being subjected. Instead of light and hope within, there began to descend a peculiar darkness and spiritual hopelessness. Sometimes I even wondered secretly if perhaps in some obscure, unknown way I might have committed the ultimate "unpardonable sin," about which the preacher prattled so much.

One thing was certain. I was dismayed by this kind of Christianity. It might suit some highly emotional temperaments but not mine.

Looking back now over 40 years of time, it stills my soul and awes my spirit to realize how patient is our God in dealing with those of us twisted and torn by all sorts of diverse teaching and preaching. Amid the confusion of church beliefs and denominational differences Christ still calls out a people for Himself. His work is often made more difficult, not easier, by the complexity of conflicts within the community of Christians.

As has been so well said, so often, "He does His own gracious, wondrous work in spite of us—not because of us." The irrepressible wind of His Spirit still moves through the midst of His people, no matter how odd some of the members may be.

This was a profound principle I learned in the little northern community that summer. Not all the people in that church were peculiar. Some were sterling souls, refined and pure as shining silver. Several became dear friends to me amid the mayhem of my inner anguish.

I found that no matter the denomination, no matter the twisted emphasis on certain doctrines, God has His own special, dear, chosen children in every church group. Often they are the least vocal, the least ostentatious, the least obvious. Yet in their quiet, gentle, gracious manner they are the ones who truly know Christ and walk with Him in calm confidence.

One young couple, who lived not far from the farm, were of this caliber. Like myself they were keen outdoor people. They loved the northern woods, the shining lakes, the abundant wildlife of the wilderness. They found inspiration, uplift and enormous enthusiasm in the pageantry of the passing seasons and the glory of the natural world around them.

As often as it was possible, I would slip away from the farm to spend an hour or two in their company. We would hike through the woods, gather the rich wild berries of summer, watch the deer feeding in the forest clearings or trace the flight of a hawk cutting wide circles in the cloud-dappled skies.

The couple were big-framed, robust, hearty, happy people. We would laugh merrily and tell tales around a crackling campfire—they of their beloved northland, and I of my sun-drenched days back in Africa's bush.

Beautiful bonds of mutual respect and devotion were built between us that summer that have endured for more than forty years.

One tremendous truth that came to me with special renewed clarity that season on the farm, was that in the outdoor world my heavenly Father had supplied a sweet solace for a struggling soul like mine. There was healing for my inner hurts in the quietness of the woods and fields. There was a consolation for my spirit in the wild glory of grass and birds and even my beloved collie friend. This dear dog, just a short time before my leaving the farm, was killed by a passing vehicle before my eyes, as we brought home a load of hay. I buried him with great tenderness.

As the bright autumn colors flamed in the northern forest

I collected my summer's wages, then slipped away for several days of respite at a rustic lakeside cottage. The tough old gent for whom I had worked so hard, in a final gesture of good will gave me a pair of pants as a bonus. I had won his respect in spite of our differences. All was well!

That fall was an unforgettable interlude. During the balmy Indian-summer days, with the skies brilliant blue, I would paddle a canoe across the lake. Its waters were crystal clear— not yet contaminated by the scourge of acid rain. The surface was like a shining mirror casting back perfect reflections of the red maples and white birches on its banks.

Here was complete peace, utter stillness, superb integration of the earth and man. The only sounds were the cry of the loons across the water, the honking of the geese overhead flying south, the swift wing-beat of ducks in full flight.

In the stillness of that setting the reassurance from God that came to me again was: "The earth is still beautiful. My presence shall go with you. Not all of life has been twisted and contorted by man and his folly. No matter where you go, I am there."

My spirit was at rest again.

Solitude and serenity had provided the strength to face another college year. My sanity had been spared from the oppression of the awful summer strain.

Looking back in retrospect, the farm interlude can perhaps be best summed up in one of my favorite amusing anecdotes:

An aged Quaker owned a beautiful Ayrshire cow whom he loved to milk at the end of his daily chores.

One evening she became rather cantankerous. First she flicked her tail around her owner's face. Then she kicked the bucket a bit. In patient tenderness he gently moved her leg back and went on milking, never uttering a single complaint. Bye and bye she stomped her feet angrily and plunged one hoof right in the pail, upsetting most of the milk on the floor.

Quietly the old farmer, without anger or oaths, stood up and set his milking stool against the wall.

Walking around her he stood facing his friend. Firmly he took her two shapely horns in his strong, gnarled hands and looked fondly into her big luminous eyes.

"Cow," he said very softly, "thou dost know I love thee

very much!" She cocked her ears forward listening to his soothing voice.

"And, cow, thou dost know that because I am a Quaker I would never get angry with thee or curse thee!" She began to chew her cud contentedly.

He went on talking to her, "Cow, thou dost also know that because I am a Quaker I would never beat thee or abuse thee."

The big, beautiful beast seemed sweetly reassured by the farmer's low, well-modulated voice.

Then he added, this time rather firmly and forcibly, "But one thing thou dost not know, cow, is this—I can sell thee to a Baptist!"

Of course, one can insert any denomination wished in this humorous story. But it illustrates pointedly the complexity of the year spent on that rock-girt farm of the far north. From it I learned a mighty lesson about genuine, godly love.

The Lure of the Mountains

THE REMAINDER OF MY YEARS at University were marked by two pronounced trends in my thinking. Steadily and significantly my studies were imbuing me with that pronounced intellectual pride of the scientific community. A certain academic haughtiness, which can become so much a part of higher education, began to make insidious inroads into my outlook on life.

Like so many of my mentors, men who knew not God, I was coming to the conclusion that given enough men, enough time, enough money and enough research, answers could be found for any dilemma facing the human race. There really is nothing quite as dangerous as only partial knowledge. Little did I realize my feet were being set on the slippery path which could easily lead me down into both spiritual and philosophical despair.

Because of my extensive studies in the fields of botany, zoology, biochemistry, bacteriology, vertebrate embryology and soil science, constant exposure to evolutionary concepts was inevitable. This was true whether in the lecture halls or research laboratories.

If a person pursues this theory of origins into the realm of human behavior, then the philosophical implications are horrendous. It is very much more than a mere matter of evolution versus creationism, as so many Christians suppose.

Rather, it becomes a question of destiny and deportment of the entire human race upon planet earth.

Either man has been created in the likeness of God, with the incredible capacity to know God, to love Him, to enjoy Him, to walk with Him and to be conformed to His character, or he has not. The evolutionary hypothesis holds that there is no creator, no God, no higher life form than homo sapiens. Man is the ultimate, highest intellectual being to appear on the planet.

This being the case, the inevitable conclusion must be that man is not responsible to any higher authority. He need not live or move or behave within any given frame of reference except that of his own design. His code of moral conduct and standards of social behavior are those of his own devising. In short, he need not be governed by God, for there is no god, except that of his own imagining. Each individual in essence becomes a god unto himself, free to do as he may wish, no matter how damaging or destructive the consequence to his contemporaries.

Ultimately it is the jungle *(evolutionary)* law of survival of the fittest which prevails. It is not the law of God implanted in man's spirit which decides his destiny or his deportment in the community of man.

This, at heart, is the essential taproot of all sophisticated, cynical scientism. It explains the universal explosion of human ideologies set against God, be they mild agnosticism, outright atheism, haughty humanism, crafty communism or hellish hedonism.

It has been in the lecture halls, the libraries, and the research laboratories of higher institutions of learning that the ideologies of despair and destruction were spawned. Our universities have become the cruel cradles of unbridled unbelief in which the malleable minds of young men and women were molded into modern infidelity.

And this pronounced process was at work on me.

It is an inevitable, inescapable impact made upon any young person exposed to university life.

Are we surprised that faith in God and confidence in Christ begin to erode and disintegrate on college campuses? Many Christian parents, in their avid eagerness to educate their

children, seldom give thought to the cataclysmic consequences of so-called higher education on their offspring.

Though my courses on campus did not include sociology
or human philosophy, favorites with so many young people
today, I was later to learn how equally diabolical they can
be. For one need not just study the scientific disciplines to
have his reverence for God destroyed. The process can be
equally potent and destructive in the humanities.

For there the concept is that man is not a tripartite being,
formed in the image of God. He is stated to be only a dual
individual with body and mind (person). It is denied that
he has a spirit or can commune with a supernatural spirit
in the person of the living God who is Spirit. It is taught
that because man is the end product of his heredity and
environment he really is not responsible for his actions or
behavior, no matter how beastly they may be.

Are we surprised, then, to see society in such chaos? Are
we appalled by the tendency to violence, crime and mayhem
in the world? Are we puzzled by the disintegration of human
dignity, the decay of human decency, the degradation of human standards? Is it any wonder the law is laughed at?

The high, noble, lofty, lovely laws of the Lord have been
exchanged for the low, lusting impulses of unregenerate man.
Yet people scream and cry, "What has gone wrong?"

The answer is simple. The eternal God of all goodness
and righteousness and justice has been spurned and repudi-
ated. In His place man has erected his own idols of self-
indulgence, self-gratification, self-assertion and self-glorifica-
tion.

The universal shout of modern man, as ever it has been
of all men of all ages, remains: "We will not have this One
to govern us—away with Him!"

Men in their folly, their darkness, their self-deception have
ever determined to do their own thing.

The consequences have always been catastrophic.

The history of the human race is a story of disgrace.

And the story of my own soul was equally fraught with
fearsome foreboding. It was being set against God.

To his eternal credit it must be said here that the one,
lone Christian professor on campus did his best to deter
my dangerous decline. He saw my dire need for spiritual

support as an overseas student. He knew communication with my own family so far away was crippled, well nigh cut-off, by wartime conditions. So he would invite me to his home for quiet visits and serious talks.

I appreciated his concern and genuine compassion. But what dismayed me was the realization that it cost him a great deal to be a Christian professor among his peers on campus. Though a brilliant scientist with a splendid record of long service, he was often passed up for promotion. He was scorned by his associates because of his bold, brave stand for righteous behavior. He was the butt of cruel jokes and snide sarcasm.

Already in my own short life I had endured enough of that sort of treatment. I was not enthusiastic for more of the same in Canada. And so I began to shy away from Christian contacts and Christian associates.

Coupled with this trend was a growing, formidable, yes, even ferocious determination for personal freedom. This intense and all-consuming preoccupation with private independence and individual initiative became a burning passion. It was a rock-hard resolve of will and mind and emotions that dominated all my desires.

Like a gyrocompass locked on the pole star, I had set my will to be my own man—to do my own thing, to realize my own aims and ambitions no matter what the cost. Any individual who does this becomes a formidable force not to be diverted or deflected from the destiny of his own choosing.

And the gentle wind of God's Spirit, though He surround such a soul and play upon such a spirit, is more often than not spurned, ignored and grieved away.

The grinding months of drudgery and tedious labor on the farm convinced me I would never again work for others for a mere pittance. I determined in those hot hay fields and stinking manure pits that I would never ever sign a contract for my labor or commit myself to terms of service which bound me to drudgery or cramped my freedom of action.

The thought began to trickle through to me that just as I had to fight ferociously with my fists as a teenager to survive in school, now in my early twenties I would have to struggle and scrap and scheme financially to overcome other obstacles and handicaps.

I determined that in ten years, by the time I was thirty, I would own my own ranch, run my own outfit, and thumb my nose at anyone who dared to deter my drive for total independence. I would ride high in the saddle and no one would dare to tell me what to do—not even God.

With such strong sentiments surging through my soul I became a hot-blooded, hard-headed young man. In short order I set out in my quest for conquest. The east with its conservative social milieu was too constricting, too set in its ways—too closed and restrictive a society to suit my rambunctious spirit.

I would head west, out to the sweeping plains, the open range of the great ranchlands, the beckoning high country of the majestic mountain ramparts. There were elbow room and wide open spaces and new opportunities for a young fellow to test his mettle and make his mark on the world.

In the early '40s much of the west was still frontier rangeland. Jets and freeways and the great migrations of ex-servicemen after the war had not yet changed the complexion of the land lying beyond the shining mountains of snow and ice. It was still largely untouched, untamed and uncrowded.

There I could carve out a kingdom for myself. There I would secure a spot in the sun. There I would succeed in finding financial security. There I would be free as the wind off the snowy ranges.

I borrowed enough money the second summer to buy a reliable used car and with my last few dollars in pocket set off for Wyoming.

As long as I live I will not forget my first view of the Rockies. It was an experience never to be duplicated for the impact of power it conveyed. I had driven relentlessly across the Midwest, across the corn fields of Illinois, Iowa and Nebraska. I rationed myself to a spartan diet of one bare meal of bread and baloney per day to save money for gas. I slept under the stars by the side of the road rolled up in a single thin blanket. I drove long hours to make maximum mileage.

Then, one dawn, I awoke at last, to look west and see the shining ramparts of the Rockies, stretched from north to south, like silver sentinels on the skyline reflecting the rising sun. The sight thrilled me so, I was unashamedly moved to tears. All alone, standing there on the edge of the sweeping prairies, I knew at last that I had come to the land of my dreams.

What I did not know was just how tough and terrible would be the struggle to see those dreams come to life. Not that the years ahead would be all toil and strain, for in fact they were to be shot through with enormous excitement, heart-stirring adventures and blood-tingling episodes—but that in it all I was gradually forgetting God in my determined drive for self-fulfillment.

Somehow, in their own unique and majestic way the western mountains cast their special spell upon me. Perhaps in part it was because of my Swiss ancestry. My forebears had been the fiercely independent hunters and herdsmen of the high Alps. No doubt wild called to wild within me. For I knew of a surety that somehow, somewhere, someway I would one day own and operate my own ranches in this wondrous western region.

All my concerted efforts to find employment on ranches in the mountain states failed. No big outfits wanted a "green-horn" on their crew. My money dwindled away. My stomach became pinched and gaunt and grim for lack of food. Finally at the verge of desperation, I landed a job building thirty-two miles of barbed-wire fence on a cattle spread in California's coastal mountains. My fellow laborers were Mexican "wet-backs" and grizzled "Okies" from the Ozark hills.

One of these dear old men was a devout Christian. He insisted on dragging me off to his two-bit church on Sunday. But I was not half as interested in the sermons as finding better ways to make more money in a hurry.

From the ranch I went to the lemon groves. Rapidly I advanced in the industry. From scraping empty boxes, stained by rotten fruit, to chief shipper I leaped from job to job in rapid promotion. By mid-summer my financial resources were flourishing. Though I have always despised money and people's preoccupation with it, I quickly learned its power, how to use it wisely, manage it skillfully, and invest it to advantage.

Two elderly Quaker ladies had given me room and board in exchange for doing all their yard work and household chores in my off-hours. Their sweet spirits, their gentle man-

ners and their huge country-cooked meals quickly restored
my own mental stability as well as strength of youthful body.

I might have remained there to become fat and flourishing,
but the snow-capped mountains had won my wild spirit. So,
with pockets bulging with cash, a friend and I took off for
western Washington, ultimately finding work on a forestry
crew working the ridges around Mount Rainier.

The rest of that late summer season seemed like pure para-
dise for me. On the alpine slopes above timber line, amid
the shining glaciers and snowfields I had found heaven on
earth. No need to talk to me about "pie in the sky." My
spirit literally sang all through that heady interlude in the
high country.

Our tent camp was situated beside a rushing, rumbling
mountain torrent that tumbled from the toe of a mighty glacier on the mountain. The atmosphere under the swaying
spruce and hemlock trees was sweet and pungent with the
aroma of upland air. We were fed the finest of fare—gigantic
meals of steaks, chops, roasts, pies, fresh-baked bread and
delicious vegetables. Our work took us up the trails and
slopes where sweeping vistas of tumbled ranges stretched
away to the blue horizon.

For a vigorous, energetic, eager youth this was a realm
of enormous inspiration, of tremendous stimulation, of
dreaming great dreams. I knew then with absolute surety
that my future would somehow be partly interwoven with
wildlife, the mountains, forests and all the splendor of their
native majesty.

In wondrous ways the mountain days helped to heal the
wounds and anguish of the previous summer. The camp com-
mander promoted me to field foreman, begging me to be
sure and return the following spring.

In His mercy and love God had arranged for one other
Christian youth to join our crew. We were drawn together
at once like two brothers. We had the same zestful enthusiasm, the same hilarious sense of humor, the same intense
love of the outdoors.

On weekends when most of the gang left for the lowland
town to blow their money on booze and brothels, he and I
would head for the highest rock ridges. There we stalked
the bears, the wild mountain goats, the deer and the coyotes.

There we drank from ice-fed springs. There we wandered wild and free over the alpine meadows now turning gold with their first touches of frost.

God had given me a life-long friend.

He had also given me golden memories to last the rest of my days.

My heavenly Father had given me a stirring preview of heaven on earth. He had spoken to me in accents I clearly understood. He had touched me deeply.

The End of Study

BY THE TIME I finally returned to University for my third year of studies my life had become imbued with twin forces of immense import to my whole future. First I had tasted personal freedom—the sort of freedom for which the United States of America has become world famous. The freedom of personal choice; the freedom of initiative; the freedom of action; the freedom of self-expression; the freedom of dreaming great dreams, then setting about to fulfill those dreams.

It was heady wine for a young man to taste in his early twenties. It was an intoxication of self-realization. It was the stuff on which empires are built by men in their quest for power.

What I did not know, and what it would take me almost twenty years to discover, was that my supposed fierce freedom was in fact but another form of insidious slavery to my own selfish self-interests . . . if it was not exercised within the context of Christ's control.

The second formidable force that had intruded itself into my whole life style was the "success syndrome." When I left campus in spring it had been as an obscure overseas student literally destitute, in search of a job. Late that autumn I returned overflowing with self-confidence and adequate financial resources to cover the cost of my courses.

My classmates could scarcely credit the record of my time

"abroad." I had traveled well over 8000 miles all across, then up and down, the western United States. I had sold the car in Seattle for profit enough to cover both the loan to buy it, as well as all my actual travel expenses. I had expanded the range of my working experience beyond my wildest dreams. I had earned wages and income few of my fellow students had ever thought possible. And my encounters with the wonderland of the mountains had made an indelible mark on me. I had become a "mountain man."

Interwoven with all of these exciting escapades, of which only the barest outline has been given in this book, was an amazing sense of adventure . . . of electric enthusiasm . . . of personal pleasure.

In a rather vague, remote manner I was aware that God, my Father, had His hand upon my affairs. Nor was I totally unmindful that dad and mother, in far-off Kenya, at the other side of the planet were praying earnestly for their boy. Few indeed were the letters between us in those war-torn years. But dad, especially, was worldly-wise enough to know his son was out in the world "feeling his oats," like a high spirited bronco not yet branded, tamed nor broken to saddle.

From the occasional letter which did reach home my parents knew full well of my new exposure to all sorts of men from all strata of society. My work on the great cattle spreads, the citrus ranches, the fire-fighting lines, the forestry crews threw me shoulder to shoulder with tough, crusty, godless men. Endless profanity, lewd language, drunkenness and debauchery were all part of the world of frontiersmen with whom I worked.

Because I was frequently the only fellow around who was still sober and able to stand on my feet, it fell to me to drag the drunks into the shower to help sober them up. I saw men squander their money in huge sums on booze and "broads." Ranch hands, fire-fighters and forestry crews were "ripe plums" plucked by pimps and prostitutes.

By the time I was twenty-two I had seen more of life than many men have at seventy-two. Much of the seamy side repulsed me. But that of prowess and power and personal pride mesmerized my surging soul.

At the college the staff of the student paper insisted I submit a write-up on my western interlude. It was to be illustrated with a selection of photographs from the pictures I had taken with a compact little camera on my travels. I worked on the article with enormous enthusiasm. Little did I realize, when it broke out in print on the front page as a feature item, that it was in fact the beginning of a literary career that would eventually encircle the whole earth.

Not only did the write-up generate great interest on campus, it also served to fuel the fires of personal pride and sinister self-esteem. Perhaps, after all, I was in the process of becoming a "self-made" man. Such nonsense and such arrogance often begin with tiny, apparently benign events in a man's career.

What I did not then realize was the conditioning of Western culture to which my character was being subjected. And, sad to say, in the inner struggle of soul and anguish of spirit which were to mark my life later, the crucial battleground was this area of self-centeredness, self-determination, self-fulfillment where there was tough reluctance to actually relinquish control of my will to Christ.

One simply cannot be "king in his own castle" and claim also to be subject to the sovereignty of God's Spirit. One cannot be a dictator deciding one's own career and conduct, while insisting that Christ is Lord in one's life. This is an outright contradiction of terms. Yet most North Americans live in the limbo of this duplicity and self-deception. Few indeed are the leaders in our pulpits with sufficient courage or conviction to dissuade their people from following such duplicity.

For the next twenty years the paths I pursued led me ever deeper into the wilderness of divided loyalties, divided drives. All the time I claimed rather lamely to be a Christian—a Christ-man—while all the time being an ardent "Kellerman"—doing my own thing in my own way.

Meanwhile the war in Europe had exploded into a full-scale global conflict. Hitler's awesome Panzer divisions had overrun most of Europe. Darkness and despair began to put out the lights of civilization all over the earth.

In furious reaction Great Britain and the Commonwealth launched a desperate counterattack on Germany from the air. The incredible victories of the Commonwealth airmen stirred the whole free world. And Churchill declared, "Never have so many owed so much to so few!"

Youths from Australia, South Africa, New Zealand, Rhodesia and a score of other countries poured into Canada for intensive air training. Our campus dormitories were taken over for barracks. Students and airmen shared the lecture rooms which now served double duty.

We agricultural students were clearly advised by the authorities that our role in food production was our first and foremost responsibility to the giant war effort. For it was the grain, the meat, the dairy products, the fruit off Canada's fields and farms that sustained most of the men in combat across the Atlantic.

A remarkable supply line of Canadian convoys, shepherded by grim, gray Corvettes, shuttled a constant stream of supplies across the cruel north Atlantic to bolster the free world's bulwark in Britain.

All us students were inducted into military training. Our gray-haired commanding officer recognized at once that I was a fully trained, combat-ready infantryman, as a result of my years in boarding school. He promptly offered me a commission. I turned it down because I despised the rules and regimentation of military command.

I had promised myself that if ever I entered the services, it would be as an intelligence officer, free to move on my own initiative. I was not prepared to forfeit my life because of other men's folly or mistakes.

Besides this I had won the coveted award on campus for rifle marksmanship. The old skills of shooting with deadly accuracy learned as a lad in Africa had never left me. So I was not prepared to go out and serve as mere gun fodder, sacrificed in wholesale slaughter under raw, unskilled army command . . . such as happened to the Canadian forces at Dieppe.

The upshot was that I again wore a uniform and bore a weapon with reluctance. But when the year's end came, instead of going to army camp I elected to head west again and work on several fine ranches in the Alberta foothills. I was convinced I could contribute more to the war effort producing cattle and wheat for men in battle, than polishing boots and bayonets in base camp.

It was on those Alberta livestock ranches in the shadow of the Rockies that I learned to ride and break horses. It was there I was introduced to the large scale use of power equipment, machinery and huge tractors for crop production. It was there I developed my own natural gifts for land management and love for fine livestock breeding. These came to me easily, comfortably and with enormous enthusiasm.

More than ever I was determined to own my own spread. I learned to cherish the land with a terrifying intensity. No day was long enough to achieve all that I wished to accomplish. I flung myself into ranching with unbridled exuberance. The result was that by the year's end the owner of the "FLYING E" outfit where I worked reported that it was his best season ever. He and his wife begged me to return after graduation and take over full operation of the spread. For now I was fully at home with registered Herefords, high quality Arabian horses, and registered seed crops.

Out in those beautiful rolling foothills, against the glorious backdrop of the Rockies on the skyline, there had been little time for God. My work had become my latest "god." Land use and land development became an absolute obsession. I was literally in love with this new field of opportunity.

Not once, in all the time I lived on those ranches both that year and the next, did I even go near a church. The land was my new love. I loved it with all my mind, heart, soul and strength.

Though I lacked any finances to purchase a property of my own, I began to inquire quietly about the possibility of picking up a small place for myself. The foothills had captured my affections. As I rode my spirited mounts across the range in the soft twilight of autumn I hoped against hope that some day it would be "Springtime in the Rockies" for me.

At last my senior year of studies was under way. One thing the time at university had taught me was that I was a man who much preferred the thrust and thrill of outdoor life to any career in academics. Books, lectures, laboratories and libraries all had their place, but I was too wild and untamed a spirit ever to be bound by the ivory-tower mentality of the university world.

Several of my professors, because of my academic performance, had approached me discreetly to see if I would consider accepting a lectureship after graduation. But the very thought of such bondage was abhorrent. I turned down their offers, much to their dismay.

About midway through the last year I had a very vivid

dream that dad died. I had not heard from home for months. Yet the last letter had indicated he was well and vigorous.

When I was suddenly called from the lecture hall the next morning I knew the reason before ever the registrar handed me the terse telegram from mother. Dad's work on earth was done. He had literally laid down his life for the Africans he loved so deeply. At the early age of fifty-four his call home had come. Africa had lost a friend. Mother had lost her beloved. And I had lost my hero!

The gracious Spirit of God, in tender compassion for my grief, had come in the night to prepare me for this sudden shattering event. Again God in Christ revealed to me vividly His own validity and living reality. For even though in recent months I had completely neglected any contact or communion with Christ, He was still there to cushion the shock of this crisis in my career.

Surely in wondrous consolation the Wind of His presence had moved completely around the planet to encircle me with His own unique comfort and compassion.

In a spontaneous outburst of selflessness, rare for me at that time, I promptly volunteered to forfeit my college career. Though I was only a few short months from graduation I would gladly have given it up to return to Kenya and pick up the work dad had laid down. Somehow I was sure this was God's will and wish for me.

Those spiritual leaders from whom I sought counsel in this matter dissuaded me from doing so. They said it was much more important to complete my studies and obtain my degree.

I accepted their advice. Yet it set a dangerous and most damaging precedent in my life. *My* work, *my* studies, *my* interests took priority over God's work, God's people, God's interests in the world.

Not until I was well past forty would those twisted priorities ever be put right in my life again. I had been set even more surely on a painful path by those who were supposed to be my leaders in the Lord.

Graduation day finally came. Dad was not there. Mother was not there. Several friends and relatives did come. One was my dad's brilliant brother from Buffalo, New York, a pastor of one of the largest churches in that city.

His eyes filled with tears. He was unable to restrain himself from weeping. For out of the seven highest honors bestowed on the graduates that day, three were claimed by his nephew, the tough, hard-headed young roustabout from the African bush. It was the climax to my early formal education.

Desperate Days

As MENTIONED EARLIER, the offers made to me at university to become a lecturer were turned down simply because I abhorred the idea of spending my life inside a building. But beyond this I had seen enough of petty politics, personal rivalry between professors, and the endless jockeying for prestige which makes up so much of the academic world.

Little did I then realize that one of the special gifts with which God had endowed me was the art of teaching. My classmates often came to my room in the evenings, asking me to explain complex subjects. Over and over they assured me that I had a unique capacity to make difficult ideas clear and easily understood. Many of them urged me to go into education. My response was to brush it off with a laugh.

More than twenty years would pass before I began to use this capacity for the benefit of others in Bible studies all over the world.

Yet the irony of it was that I desperately wanted to share what knowledge and experience were mine. And this I felt could best be done in some sort of extension work in the field of agriculture or resource conservation.

There were very promising and in those days lucrative openings for this service in the Canadian government. The officials came to the campus to interview interested graduates. To my utter horror, anger and dismay I was turned down every time. Not because I was incompetent—my honors and experience proved otherwise—but because I was foreign-born.

Discrimination had again reared its ugly visage. I was furious. A fierce, vicious type of sinister bitterness began to infiltrate my attitude to life.

I had worked so hard, studied so diligently and given every ounce of concentration to attaining outstanding success in my university training. Now none of it seemed of any value. What good was a degree in science with honors—without a job?

It seemed the ancient adage had come true: "It is not what you know that counts—But who you know!"

This was an aspect of society that made my youthful blood boil. I saw second-rate students who had frittered away their four years find excellent positions in trade, industry or research simply because their parents had influence or knew the proper people. I saw graduates with the "right connections" land cozy appointments while I landed out on the open road with no promise of employment.

I began to be very antisocial. An intense distrust of humanity began to harden within my spirit. I started to despise the so-called system that showed so much partiality to the favored few.

Though some friends and relatives attempted to "go to bat on my behalf" it all seemed of no avail. I was still a stranger in a stern land where only the very tough could ever get to the top.

In my anger, frustration and black bitterness I determined I would go west again. Perhaps I could catch a ship on the Pacific coast that would carry me back to Africa. If Canada did not want me, at least I could survive in the Kenya bush.

Too proud to ride the rails again as I had the previous spring in going to the foothill ranch, I pawned what few possessions I had, bought a train ticket and headed for Alberta. At least I would ride in a coach and not a cattle car. I was too proud to hitchhike across country as I had done the summer before.

As the train rolled west, the steady drum of its wheels on the rails beat a hardening shell of resentment around my spirit. I felt utterly forlorn. I seemed to be abandoned. There was no place to turn. All that I could do in desperation was try to find work.

In Calgary all my efforts to obtain employment, other than that of a ranch hand, failed. The same old reason. Foreign-born.

Finally in utter futility I hitchhiked back down to the ranch where I had worked the previous year. The boss was glad to have me back. But I was less than happy.

The spring season had been late. Seeding was behind. The ranch operation was somewhat in disarray, and I was somehow expected to put it all right.

I did.

With my usual tremendous drive I broke several new horses to harness, and "mudded in" the whole crop with a four-horse outfit, able to work the land where all the heavy tractors bogged down.

In the same way, by skillful management and long hours of labor, we put up the only good stacks of hay harvested in that area during the unusual wet season.

By late summer the ranch was in first-class order. A fine crop of grain promised enormous autumn yields. Huge hay stacks were a sure guarantee against winter. And a prime crop of registered Brome seed was ready for harvest.

One evening, after supper, I decided to tackle the rancher about my future. I was not content to remain a mere hired hand the rest of my life. If I was to stay on his spread I wanted a working partnership in the business and a legitimate share in the profits that my expertise produced.

His operation had become the talk of the community.

Neighboring ranchers were astounded at our success.

They knew full well the difference lay in my management.

The rancher and his wife were adamant in their refusal to give me any share in the operations. They had a good thing going and did not want it any different.

Suddenly my pent-up frustration and bitterness blew like a volcano of vituperation and violence. All the anger, all the animosity, all the hostility of my inner hate flamed white-hot.

A stream of appalling profanity, cursing and swearing erupted out of my soul. In blind rage I demanded all my wages. The next day at dawn I hit the road for the mountains to the west.

I arrived on the Pacific coast in a downpour of rain that flooded every street and storm drain. The deep, dark overcast exactly matched my own desperate, miserable mood. I did not know a single soul in British Columbia, a region larger than all of California, Oregon and Washington combined.

All that stood between me and utter desperation was a mere $120.00 stuffed in my work-worn wallet.

Where would I turn now?

What did a man do in such straits?

Why had life turned so sour?

At such moments it is not hard to turn to crime.

I was a rabid, rebellious, angry young man who was incensed enough at society to resort to violence to survive.

If life was to be this tough, then I, too, could play it rough. I was not about to be cowed by the world in which I was unwanted, unknown, unaccepted.

At night I slept on the hard wooden benches in the old railway station down by the docks. The railway police periodically routed me out to go and tramp along skid row.

I roamed the Vancouver waterfront trying to find some ship that would sign me on as a deck hand. But no one would have me. The war with Japan raged across the Pacific and every seaman was under careful surveillance.

My few dollars were dwindling to nothing.

The only job I had been offered was sweeping floors in a stinking slaughterhouse. This I was too proud to take . . . too angry to even consider.

Then as now I could see clearly why a society in which troubled youths are unable to find employment because of race, color or discrimination is ever prone to violence and crime. Beneath its surface there simmers sinister vengeance.

Only by the mercy of God was I plucked from taking that last perilous step which would have plunged me over the precipice of personal vengeance into a vicious life of crime.

Just as my last few dollars were about to vanish I stumbled into a job as an expeditor in a local aircraft plant. Boeings of Seattle had set up a Canadian plant at Sea Island to build the famous PBY Flying boats, used extensively for submarine patrol.

In short order I found room and board with an aged, retired gentleman whose hobby was cooking. His meals were superb. And once again my pinched frame filled out on his splendid fare.

What did not turn out so well was his passionate homosexuality. It took dogged will power to resist his advances. Finally he learned I would have absolutely nothing to do with his disgusting behavior.

This alienation seemed to sharpen and intensify my loneliness. There is no spot on earth quite as forbidding as a rainy, fog-shrouded seaport in winter, where there is no one to turn to as a friend.

Driven by desperation I decided one night to attend a large church where special services were being held. It seemed a long, long time indeed since I had entered a sacred sanctuary.

Amid my anger and hostility I had literally turned my back on God. In the fury of my frustration I felt He really had not been concerned about my plight. And as I bungled my way through life in bewilderment I blamed Him for my dilemma.

That night in that church deep conviction came over me because of my crude conduct and atrocious attitudes to both God and men. In the bright, intense light of God's Word I perceived myself as a prodigal. In profound penitence and genuine remorse I turned again to Christ, seeking reconciliation.

In a very real sense this could be regarded as a second conversion. It was a crisis as critical and crucial as when I first sought salvation as a small lad.

It was the typical inner trauma of a person who in desperation turns to the church for solace and comfort in the hour of darkest need. What I did not then realize was that in a peculiar and perverse way I was accepting Christ and His forgiveness in an intellectual way. I was reestablishing rapport with Christians as a social convenience to find friends and human support.

My initial conversion as a boy had been emotional.

My second conversion and recommitment as a young man to Christ was intellectual and social. I even consented to be baptized a second time!

It would still be another twenty years before the mainspring of my tough will was truly touched by God. Only then would I discover what it was to really know Him in truth and walk with him in humble obedience.

True to form I quickly found friends. One young Scottish

youth became a close companion. His widowed, loving mother was like a second mother to me. She took me into her heart and into her home. From her there flowed to me the love and warmth of personal, caring human kindness I had craved for so long.

At last it looked as if life did have a silver lining within its dark thunder clouds. The sun did shine again. And the good days did outnumber the bad.

After an interlude of nearly seven years I picked up the violin once more. With my very first pay-check in pocket I went in search of someone to give me lessons.

Because I had so many evenings alone there was enormous opportunity to practice. To my teacher's delight I made remarkable progress. And in a few months he invited me to join the Vancouver Symphony.

Then suddenly my whole, strange, rather unreal, citified world caved in.

A formidable letter from the authorities in Ottawa arrived in the mail one day. They had found out I was employed in the aircraft plant. I had no right to be there. I was an agricultural scientist and was obliged to be in wartime service in my special field. I was to quit my job and seek employment in my own discipline.

The telegram I sent back to the Wartime Control Board in Ottawa was so heated and angry it almost scorched the paper on which it was scribbled.

If the Canadian government insisted on my serving in a field of their choice, then indeed they would have to provide the opening. I adamantly refused to relinquish my job until they supplied me with a substitute.

Several months later a second letter came. I was to transfer to the experimental and research station at Agassiz. This little village lying amid the orchards and farms of the famous Fraser Valley would be my headquarters for the duration of the war. My major responsibiltiy was to do crop and soil research for the Province of British Columbia.

Once again my roots were being torn up by people and events over which I had no control. The crude, bare room in the old, barnlike boarding house at the experimental station would be my seventeenth residence since I had left my parents' humble home at the age of eight.

At times I felt like a bit of flotsam flung about on the tempestuous tides of time. One month here, the next there. Often as I strolled along the village streets looking into the little yards and curtained windows, I wondered if ever I would even own a home of my own. Was it a dream too good to ever come true?

A peculiar inner longing, a deep yearning to "belong" began to obsess me. Perhaps prayer might just change things.

Serious, earnest prayer was something I knew little about.

Romance

JUST A FEW WEEKS before leaving the city, my chum had prevailed upon me to attend a home Bible study with him. In those days such groups were rather uncommon—not like now, where thousands of such classes are held all over the country.

It is with a sense of personal contrition I confess that I agreed to go, more or less just to humor my friend. Bible study seemed, to a sophisticated young scientist like myself, a bit of a bore. Though mother, in her compassionate concern for me as a young man, had presented me with a beautiful, expensive study Bible when I left home, it had been buried in the bottom of my old battered trunk, never opened.

At the classes I took a peculiar stance of cynicism toward the Scriptures. Their truths and teaching were challenged. I contended that they lacked credibility as a code of personal conduct for man's survival in our scientific, sophisticated society. Of course there was nothing new in this. It is not enough to just know truth in an intellectual dimension. It is then only theory, doctrine or theology.

What I had to discover much later in life was that divine truth only becomes a dynamic force in one's personal experience as it is actually lived out, acted upon and tested by trial. Then, as Jesus put it, "The words which I speak unto you, they are spirit and they are life . . ." becomes a living reality.

But the Bible classes seemed to serve a useful social function. One met stimulating people there. And it was a pleasant way to pass an evening. Most important, God was there!

Then one night it happened. My friend and I came a little late. We were obliged to be seated very close to two young ladies, sisters, both of whom were strikingly beautiful and exquisitely groomed.

The older, with shining blue eyes and a radiant countenance, captured my attention.

Her whole demeanor was delightful. She had an aura of serenity and gentle quietness that I had seldom seen expressed so superbly in a young woman.

After the class we were introduced. The few words exchanged in conversation convinced me Phyllis Wood was no ordinary lady. She was an individual of unusual Christian character.

Perhaps it would be helpful to the reader to pause here and explain a bit about the boy-girl relationships which had marked my life up to this explosive point.

Because my earliest childhood years were bereft of brothers and sisters I knew nothing of little girls. All the schools I attended were strict in their segregation of the sexes. Only the last few terms before entering high school were students at the school I attended allowed to date; there the puppy love I saw seemed absurd and silly.

In high school there were no girls at all, except the occasional ones met in a home. They simply did not seem to be of any great consequence in the life of a young fellow consumed by a fierce love for the wilds.

By the time I was through university I had lived in so many situations where homes were a hellish battleground, instead of a haven of peace, that the thought of marriage left me rather wary of women.

On the ranch there had been coy cowgirls who tried to entice me with their soft eyes and sweet smiles. But I was too preoccupied with work and dreams of owning my own spread that I did not want to be tied down by some little woman who might shortcut my ambitions.

So here I was now, a young man of twenty-four who had never even held a girl in his embrace or felt the ecstacy of a feminine kiss warm with romantic affection. In our sex-oriented society this was unusual.

The enormous attraction now generated for Phyllis was, I believe sincerely, one of those beautiful arrangements made on my behalf by a loving heavenly Father. For in my stern, spartan, severe aloneness He knew I needed a companion with whom to share life.

For the ancient saying still holds true, "Joy shared is a double delight, and sorrow shared is only half a burden."

What I did not know when first we met, was that Phyllis was just a little older than I was. Nor was I aware that because of her beautiful appearance and winsome personality she was a popular lady sought after by several dashing young suitors. At least one of these was a high-ranking military officer.

Consequently she was rather reluctant to respond to my unpolished and persistent attempts to make her better acquaintance. Finally through my sheer perseverance she agreed to go out with me for a dinner date.

When I arrived at her home to pick her up I was in mortal terror. For I had never met her parents and feared this first unknown encounter.

Knocking at the door I expected to be met by Phyllis. Instead, it was her dad who opened it. He was stripped to the waist, his strong chest and forearms muscled like those of a prizefighter. His face was lathered in thick foamy shaving soap. To a young man facing his first serious date he looked a terrifying spectacle. I half expected he held a shotgun behind his broad, burly back.

He grunted rather gruffly that I should step in, then turned swiftly to disappear into the kitchen, leaving me standing awkwardly in the hall. What I did not then realize was that he was really as nervous and embarrassed as I was.

In a few moments Mrs. Wood came down the stairs. She was a woman of remarkable beauty. Gently she apologized that Phyllis was not quite ready, then seated me in the front room.

It was the first of many visits in this unusual home. The initial impressions of her father had been dead wrong. He turned out to be a dear, humble man of tremendous integrity and quiet confidence in Christ. And Mrs. Wood was a woman of shining spirit and great goodwill.

They had four delightful daughters, who in the security and serenity of this cheerful home had enjoyed a childhood and youth of unusual tranquillity and security. The whole atmosphere of the family residence was one of genuine goodwill, good cheer, and gracious gaiety.

I had never been in such a home before. It gave me the distinct impression of being "a bit of heaven on earth"—"an oasis of serenity amid the waste of a wretched world at war." For the first time since leaving home as a small lad at eight years of age I truly felt I had found a place of peace.

It did not surprise me that Phyllis had grown up to be such an attractive, serene, well-balanced person. Not only was she beautiful in appearance but also winsome in spirit, a rare combination indeed.

Yet she was not naive. She had not been raised in a hothouse environment sheltered from the stresses and strains of society. She, too, had worked hard after graduation from high school. Her integrity, industry and self-discipline had assured her of steady advances in her career. When we met she held the responsible position of private secretary to a top executive in the publishing industry.

Much to my delight, she began to feel drawn to me. We could not see each other as often as we might have wished, for I was soon posted to the research center some seventy miles away. Yet absence makes the heart grow fonder. And despite the distance we managed to see each other on occasional weekends and holidays.

No doubt a large part of the credit for the success of our courtship lay in the prayers of our parents. Even though my widowed mother was half a world away, she never ceased to beseech God that I would find a fine life-companion. My friend's widowed mother in Vancouver who had opened her home for this wanderer was just as diligent in her prayers for my future. And of course Phyllis' own parents, being such devout people, made this romance a matter of utmost priority in their prayers. Few of us appreciate the prayers of others enough.

To their eternal credit it must be said that Mr. and Mrs. Wood never tried to manipulate our affairs. They never interfered in our decisions. They stood by us calmly with quiet strength and godly wisdom.

When at last we were about to be engaged, I felt it my honorable responsibility to request the hand of their daughter in marriage. It was to their credit she had become such a lovely lady. The least I could do was show my deep respect for their great part in the pageantry.

They gave their whole-hearted blessings to our engagement. For me this was a turning point of dramatic and dynamic consequence. At last, after so long a sojourn in angry alienation against society, I felt myself being drawn gently into the warm affectionate fabric of a human family.

Having someone to love, and being loved back in return, began to soften some of the tough, hard walls of resistance built up around my stony spirit.

It began to come home to me clearly that, after all, I was not entirely alone in the world, battling to survive. Here was someone who cared deeply about me, who really dared to share my dreams, who was willing to work hard in helping me build for an exciting future.

Suddenly life again was truly a great adventure. My soul had been touched by the compelling wind of God's Spirit who was so very active and apparent in my beloved fiancée.

Fortunate indeed is the young man who finds a life companion who truly loves God. Phyllis was not a superficial Christian. Her entire person and conduct were a characterization of Christ. She radiated the inner life of God's own gracious Spirit. And this had a profound impact on my own tough, hard disposition. She generated within me the deep desire to know God as she did, to enjoy His presence as she did in a personal, intimate manner.

The quiet, godly impact of her influence became a source of strong assurance that life could be worthwhile; it could be beautiful; it could also be romantically exciting.

All of this in spite of the spartan circumstances under which I lived and worked at the research station.

There I had been assigned to a cold drafty room in the old bunkhouse. Most of its inmates were elderly men who had struggled hopelessly through the Depression then found some meager security in this spot doing routine maintenance jobs around the station.

They were men of broken dreams, broken hopes and bitter regrets. Only the prospect of a meager government pension prevented them from packing up and moving down the road again. They were scarcely the sort of stimulating associates an ambitious young man would choose for companions. But I was stuck with them for the duration of the war. So there was no escape.

Only one individual was an exception. He was old George Brown, a crusty, tough, but passionate sheep man from the north of Scotland. He and "Glen," his remarkable sheep dog, were inseparable companions. Together they cared for the fine flock of Cheviots at the station.

George in his rough-hewn way befriended me. He would regale me with all the exciting episodes of his colorful career.

Gently but surely, in any spare time we shared, he would impart to me many of the secrets in sheep husbandry which only a lifetime of experiences could accumulate. Little did I then know how soon I would need that expertise.

The long evenings in the bunk house were a bit of a bore. Though I borrowed and read almost every book in the tiny local library, my enormous pent-up energies needed some other outlet for expression. Almost without any prompting I decided to fill in the long hours with writing.

Books had always been an immense inspiration to me. Some of my greatest heroes were authors of books who had shared their life adventures with readers through their writing and photographs. The memoirs of men like Theodore Roosevelt, Carl Akeley, Cherry Kearton and Martin Johnson stirred my spirit. They gave me the burning desire to do the same thing: travel the world, explore new terrain, study wildlife and primitive people, photograph exciting scenes, then report it all to those unable to travel themselves.

So in my spare time I began to produce a book manuscript. I worked on it for hundreds of hours. I submitted parts of it to a book editor who quietly assured me that I had an unusual gift for writing. He warned me, however, that writing was a tough discipline. It called for tremendous self-sacrifice. Yet for those who succeeded, it was an exciting field of creative worth. Above all else it demanded patient perseverance.

How much, I did not realize then. I would actually write and rewrite steadily for the next eleven years of my life before a single line was ever accepted for publication. But I had a will of steel. In that drab, drafty bunk house room, lit by only one dim, bare, thirty-watt bulb suspended from the ceiling, I determined I would one day have books bearing my name, in libraries all over the world. I locked my will on this aim like a gyrocompass fixed on the pole star.

I had set my feet on a certain course from which nothing would ever deflect me . . . even if it took thirty years to achieve it.

In my work at the station I quickly discovered an important concept. It was the peculiar work ethic of the civil service. The whole system was shot through with so-called "dead wood." Here were men and women drawn from all strata of society who had simply settled down cozily in a comfortable job, putting in time until their retirement rolled around.

Security was their main preoccupation.

Little wonder there was so little enthusiasm, energy or excitement generated in government endeavors. This wartime experience opened up the whole realm of burdensome bureaucracy to me. The redundancy, incompetence and appalling waste of money, time and personnel on petty projects astounded and dismayed me.

I had half hoped that perhaps I could carve out a career in the civil service. But such a notion was quickly jettisoned; I would have died from sheer frustration and endless ennui.

One of my fellow workers detected my unrest and increasing disenchantment with the "system." Being an avowed and ardent communist, he took every opportunity to pour his pernicious propaganda into my still malleable mind.

For hours at a stretch, as we worked together he would whisper into my ears the subtle, sinister suggestions of all the supposed advantages to be gained from socialism. I appeared ripe for such pernicious ideas. He might well have done me irreparable damage had the war not suddenly ended with the explosion of atomic bombs over Hiroshima and Nagasaki.

Not only did the blinding, burning blasts end hostilities around the world, they set me free to leave government service. I would seek a new field of endeavor in industry and commerce. Perhaps this would be the shortest, most direct path to the personal freedom and financial independence I craved so fiercely.

At Last a Home

DURING THE LONG, SLOW, grinding months that my wartime service held me at the research center, Phyllis and I laid careful plans for our future together. The warmth of her affection, the regularity of her love letters, the constancy of her prayers helped more than anything else to give great hope for a home of our own.

Careful inquiries were made about finding a position in the private sector where advancement would be much more rapid than in the civil service. After a number of interviews I decided to accept a post as seed production manager for one of the largest companies in the country.

It was to prove a tremendous challenge. For in the early, post-war period Canada had undertaken the generous rôle of supplying field and garden seed to the war-ravaged countries of Europe. Thousands of tons of registered grain and vegetable seeds were shipped, free of charge, across the Atlantic to rehabilitate the destitute and devastated farmlands of nations wrecked by the war.

In a pattern similar to that of The Marshall Plan in the United States, the victorious Canadians stretched out their hands to help the beaten and downtrodden of the earth to stand on their feet again. As a young man I felt a tremendous thrill in being a part of this generous and gracious gesture. It remains an act of goodwill seldom if ever matched in the horrendous history of mankind.

My particular rôle was to supervise the production of well over fifty varieties of seed from more than a hundred ranches scattered from the Pacific to the prairies. It was an enormous undertaking that demanded terrific drive and energy. But I was vibrantly excited with the project. I was young, charged with eager enthusiasm. Best of all, it was the means to assure our establishing a home of our own.

Phyllis and I had both saved all we could from our salaries. Because we had been so frugal it was possible to gather to-gether sufficient funds to make a substantial down payment on a cute cottage that stood on two adjoining lots. The full price by today's standards sounds unbelievable. For both beautiful lots plus the cozy home with its wide windows over-looking Vancouver's north-shore mountains the full price was $3,500.00. Our monthly payments, at 3.75% interest, amounted to $25.00, which could be waived, if things got too tough.

We were married rather quietly in a small chapel near my bride's home. The man who presided was a Christian lay worker from a nearby youth camp who had taken a special interest in our romance.

Our honeymoon was rather unusual. We boarded a small coastal steamer to a secluded island in the Gulf of Georgia. There, a rustic lodge with tiny guest cottages provided ideal accommodation for young lovers like ourselves.

We had purposely, and with great care, chosen the period of full moon in midsummer for our romantic interlude. The lodge was located on the shores of a beautiful, private sand beach. There we spent hours swimming in the sea, relaxing in the sun or strolling arm in arm under the magic spell of mellow moonlight.

There were winding trails through the nearby fields and forests. Here we wandered in joyous contentment. I would pick wild flowers and place them in Phyllis' beautiful dark hair as an added adornment to her natural beauty.

Those were precious days that passed in radiant ecstasy. Not only had I found a life mate of winsome attractiveness, but also a woman of gracious, gentle spirit, radiant with happy good humor. She was indeed a jewel of great worth!

In a very real and practical sense Phyllis and her family became my family. Her dad became my dad, the more so since my own father had passed away. Her mother became a dear friend. Her keen mind, her gay humor, her radiant optimism, her striking beauty were all attributes which elicited my ardent admiration. And the three sisters provided a wide dimension of feminine fun and pleasure I had never known as a young person. We joked, teased and enjoyed each other in a wondrous family way.

In all of this there began to break in upon my rather hard and indifferent heart the acute awareness that my Father above really had not abandoned me, even in my stormy, wayward ways. His hand had been upon me for good. He had led me to this home, to this family, to this gorgeous girl whose life would be such a force in shaping my own.

Just as the war clouds began to blow away from across the earth, so the clouds of personal despair began to dissipate from my own outlook. The wind of God's Spirit kept sweeping into my soul with fresh expectancy and bright hopes. Life could be full, rewarding and vibrant with great dreams taking shape in concrete form.

Phyllis brought a charming new dimension of softness and loveliness into our home. She was a girl without vanity or self-preoccupation. Many young women with her beautiful features and flawless complexion would have been haughty and arrogant. She was not. Her graceful carriage and lissome form were shaped and sculpted by vigorous swimming and energetic walking.

She turned our cottage into a special lovenest, not with a lot of frills and furbishes, but by exquisite good taste and the subtle touches of a warm, gentle, affectionate woman. Our home became a place of peace, an oasis of contentment, a sanctuary of serenity that enfolded us in quiet happiness.

In a deep, profound way she recognized that marriage was not a matter of confrontation or competition with her mate, but rather of cooperation. Her remarkable feminine instincts recognized her rôle as that of complementing her husband. She was fully aware that her magnetic feminine charms and exquisite loveliness, instead of being paraded for personal gratification, could be the great magnet which bound me to her as a man, proud and glad to be her friend and life companion.

She rejoiced in being my beloved.

I revelled in being her lover.

This harmony was reflected in our home. It was a haven of happiness and gracious goodwill. Even our rather crusty neighbors noticed this and commented on it. Newlyweds seldom were so readily adjusted to one another.

Perhaps in part it was because I had been without so much so long, that anything Phyllis did or provided was like a gift from heaven, for which I was so deeply grateful. She often commented on this attribute of my ardent appreciation all through our life together. It seemed to touch her deeply.

Both of us found special pleasure in the small tasks of home improvement to our property. We painted and polished the interior of the wee house until it sparkled. Outside I tore out all the weeds and debris that had accumulated across the years. A fine vegetable garden was planted. A rose bed was set out. The fruit trees were pruned and fertilized. New lawns were seeded so that soon neighbors stopped to chat, comment on the changes taking place, then went home to improve their own places.

Our ideas were contagious. Soon the entire street began to take on an improved appearance. Our real estate agent dropped by to see us and remarked that we could possibly double our money if we decided to sell.

My bride's family were devout, earnest, godly people who fellowshiped with a tiny, struggling work in the waterfront section of the city. They were an unusual group who had no pastor. The lay people ran the assembly. Women were forbidden to speak in the services. They were obliged to wear head covering. They "broke bread" together every Sunday and permitted only their own membership to partake of communion.

Because of their strict sort of service they called themselves "Brethren." In fun, and as a pun, I often called Phyllis my cistern (sistern), "my fountain of joy."

By mutual agreement we decided to attend a small, dry, little Baptist church only a couple of blocks from where we lived. We could walk there easily, and it was a spot where Phyllis was happy to teach a class of girls.

As is so often the case, the leaders were so tickled to have a new couple come to the services, they were sure I was the right person to teach a teenage boys' group. It proved to be a comedy of errors. At my stage of spiritual maturity, just then, instructing bombastic boys from the tough part of town was not to prove of much value. Churches so often make this common error.

Almost the first session we had, the local bully, a tough young roustabout, tested my will to impose discipline in the class. He clowned around, stirring up a storm among the students. My temper exploded. In a flash I literally picked him up bodily like a mastiff shaking a terrier, and tossed him out of the building, down the front steps of the church.

Fifteen minutes later he crept back into the now silent class, full of contrition and surprising respect.

My furious action horrified the whole church.

It was the last Sunday school class I ever taught. I had discovered very quickly that I had no talent for teaching teenagers.

It was at this little church that I began to grill the pastor about perplexing problems that plague anyone active in the business community. I was advancing in the company rapidly. As I assumed ever greater responsibilities for the firm I was being faced with formidable choices as to what was right and what was wrong in business ethics.

I was not a pious prude. I had packed a horrendous amount of hard-boiled living into my first twenty-five years of life; only a fraction of it has been told in this account. But it made my blood race and my temper turn white hot to see the clever tactics and tough methods used by a large corporation to impose its will on both its employees and on those with whom it did business.

I began to participate in some of the major policy-making sessions. I was invited to sit in on the special luncheon meetings at the men's business club where the head executives callously decided the direction the company would take in expanding its empire.

Maximum profits were the top priority. No matter that the little people, poor people, working people, trusting people were pushed to the wall. All that mattered was to make money, lots of it, as fast and furiously as possible. I was given a frightening, firsthand view of the brutality that can be an integral part of "big-business."

Whenever I raised my voice to protest or plead for some

degree of decency and fair play I was silenced by my superiors. The utter ruthlessness of management startled and shook me. Little wonder that in due course unions, closed shops, and angry strikes would come to be such a painful and prominent part of the volcanic social scene in British Columbia.

I tried to discuss my dilemma with the dear, gray-haired old pastor in the little corner church. But all to no avail.

He, like so many ministers, had led a safe and sheltered life. Raised in a quiet serene home, he had simply gone from high school, to Bible school, to seminary, then into the pulpit. Nowhere along the way had he faced the formidable slash and thrust of struggling to survive in the hard-boiled business community.

Most of his answers to me were simply pious platitudes, pat answers that would not work in my rough realm. I begged him for further help if it could be found elsewhere. In response he brought me a massive, weighty book on "Christian Doctrines" from his library.

That book had a devastating impact on me. I took it very seriously. I perused its pages for hours. In a peculiar way it began to raise enormous questions in my mind about the veracity and practical application of Christianity to the twentieth century. It appalled and dismayed me that diverse denominations could hold such distinct and divergent views on the same subject, all apparently supported by Scripture.

Where was truth? Who had the final answer?

How did one arrive at a definitive decision? What could one really count on as being correct?

In dismay I returned the book on doctrine. I decided then and there that the only truth which counted was that which actually worked in the rough and tumble of life. I lost all interest in the scholarly dissertations of divines who sat in their sheltered sanctuaries writing weighty tomes that were often untested theory—yet were supposed to be theology.

No wonder Jesus held the scribes and ecclesiastical hierarchy of His day in such contempt. So did I in mine!

It was a tough stance I took. Yet it was dangerous.

For in a sense it began to shut me off from searching the Scriptures for myself. The church just became a part of the social scene. I had other more important priorities to take care of.

Phyllis and I revelled in our new life together. Our quiet, joyous contentment in the home was punctuated by Saturday outings in the surrounding countryside. We spent exciting hours roaming the coast, swimming in the sea, collecting driftwood and enjoying evening fires on the beaches.

Other times we went inland on picnics and foraging excursions. We would bring home buckets of wild berries, the occasional game bird that fell to my gun, armfuls of fresh fruit, or vegetables from friendly farmers' fields.

Amid all this happiness only one small cloud of concern hovered above the horizon of our home. Heart-wrenching letters began to reach us from my widowed mother, now well advanced in years, who was still working in Kenya.

She was endeavoring valiantly to carry on her work for God. But after dad's death, advancing age, and the arrival of other missionaries, her rôle had been complicated. Increasingly she sensed a concerted attempt was being made by newcomers to supplant her. Unfortunately, as sometimes happens in such cases, misunderstandings, grievances and heartache followed.

I was not one to dismiss such injustice lightly. In fact, the abuse suffered by mother grieved me. I found it difficult to accept the abrasive stance taken by younger, so-called Christian workers toward a veteran widow who had poured out her life for Africa.

So, at my urging, it was decided she should retire from the field. In her own good time she would come to live with us until a home of her own could be established.

The Search

UP UNTIL WORLD WAR II, British Columbia, apart from its coastal cities of Vancouver and Victoria, was a vast mountain region scarcely touched by the technology of the twentieth century. An area in size equal to all of California, Oregon and Washington combined, it was a rather remote region known to most Canadians only as "the land beyond the Rockies."

A light sprinkling of audacious ranchers, miners, trappers and loggers had moved into the narrow valleys and open rangeland lying amid the mountains. With raw courage and frontier fortitude they had settled wherever land was suitable for cultivation. But because 98 percent of the province is "on edge" in gigantic folded mountain ranges, the farms and ranches were widely scattered, connected only by twisted, torturous gravel roads that wound from one community to the next.

It was a realm of remarkable natural beauty and wild untamed wilderness. Wildlife abounded. Magnificent lakes, rushing rivers and shining peaks were as yet almost virgin, unknown, untouched.

My work and my responsibilities took me throughout this entire region. From the gorgeous Pacific Coast to the rolling foothills of the Rockies that stretched to the prairies, I had a hundred farms and ranches under contract to produce seed. Every month from early spring until the end of autumn I traveled the gravel roads and dusty trails inspecting the crops, supervising production, making sure the harvest came off in prime condition, ready for final cleaning and shipment to Europe.

It was a thrilling interlude. My whole outlook and view of agricultural development expanded and widened. I was in personal, intimate contact with all sorts of ranchers, farmers and seed growers.

More fiercely than ever there was fanned within me a consuming fire of desire to own and develop a ranch of my own. I was not just content to act as a land consultant to those active in the industry. I longed, ached, dreamed of the day when I, too, could stand tall on my own wide acres and declare proudly, *"This is mine!"*

Because of my background as a boy, wild called to wild in my adventuresome spirit. The wilderness of British Columbia, the wide open ranges, the rampaging rivers, the clear limpid lakes ignited a fierce and passionate love for this lovely region.

My company recognized quickly that I was no ordinary field man, content to travel their territory, staying in the rather wretched little hotels and eating in the run-down Chinese restaurants scattered along the route. So they provided me with a powerful, high-speed car, and all the camping gear I needed to make my own accommodation along the way.

The double delight and special benefit of this very unique arrangement was that Phyllis could accompany me on all of my travels. We were two light-hearted, joyous explorers who soon found all the choicest spots to pitch a tent and make camp in this magnificent mountain region.

It is hard to realize that thirty-five years ago we would be the only people with a tent and campfire on the beach of a beautiful lake or the bank of a singing river where today there are thousands of tourists. It was a time of enormous stimulus to our souls and spirits. As a young couple we came to know each other with tremendous trust and affection in our quiet interludes when the day's work was done.

I would return from field inspection to find a fine supper prepared over an open fire. We would relish the fish I had caught, or a game bird I had shot or a roast of beef or lamb purchased from a rancher. We would lie by the fire under the shining stars munching fresh fruit from the orchards along the way.

There in the stillness of the night with moonlight turning the lakes and streams to silver we would dream dreams of owning and developing our own ranch. And so we began to search quietly for a spot that we might purchase. Perhaps we would stumble on a good piece of ground that had been abused, neglected, maybe even abandoned. At least it could be bought at a reasonable figure. Then with love, skill, hard work and modern technology it could be turned into a flourishing enterprise and happy home.

Meanwhile life was for living. Phyllis and I took full advantage of every possible opportunity my work gave us to enjoy the wild realm in which I worked. Our bodies were bronzed from long days under summer sun. Our vigor and vitality were tremendous because of all the fresh air, wholesome food and abundant outdoor exercise. Our minds and emotions were keen with eager anticipation and the high hopes which are so rich a part of youth.

Perhaps amid all the adventure and excitement of our early days together the one aspect which I tended to neglect was our spiritual growth. Not that we cut off our Christian fellowship. This never did happen. Always, ever, especially because of my bride, we had Bible reading and daily devotions after breakfast each day. But for me as a man bursting with enthusiasm for my work, spiritual values were relegated to a rather minor and unimportant role in our lives.

What I did not then realize was that steadily but surely my priorities as a man were becoming reversed. I was proudly and passionately in love with Phyllis. She had become my first love. Secondly, I was tremendously fond of the land and now searched relentlessly for a spot to claim and make my own. Thirdly, I was fascinated by the wilderness and wildlife. Increasingly I developed an enormous enthusiasm for outdoor life and resource conservation. These three, my wife, land, and wildlife became my obsessions.

Without embarrassment or apology I gave the whole of my person, strength and attention to them. Nothing else seemed of much consequence. Christianity was but a peripheral consideration, pushed out onto the extreme perimeter of my interests and thoughts.

Instead of seeking God first, I had the process exactly reversed and was intensely searching for the fulfillment of my own selfish desires. For years to follow I would leave no stone unturned, no step untrod that I thought might possibly hasten my own personal advancement. My dreams, my aims, my ambitions, my aspirations became the center of my preoccupation. Like millions upon millions of other young North Americans I had become totally egocentric. I would succeed—no matter what!

My company quickly recognized this unusual drive and energy. The management marveled at the rapid increase in production of the department under my supervision. Output soared. Profits multiplied. The company applauded. I was riding the crest of a surging wave of success. It was a "high" for one so young and so new to the industry. My salary was increased, my fringe benefits were enlarged and every prospect pleased.

Then one day the phone rang. It was the president. He wanted to see me privately in his office. I was to come for a major conference the next day.

The company had acquired magnificent holdings in some of the richest range country in the interior. They had massive plans for a major development that included land-clearing, livestock production, irrigation schemes and the manufacture of high protein feed.

Would I take over immediate responsibility for management and development? I would be given another substantial raise in pay. Free housing would be provided. Besides there would be other major benefits.

I accepted the offer. It was the chance of a lifetime.

Little did I know it was to be one of the critical turning points in my whole career.

When we arrived at the ranch it appeared as beautiful as a landscape painting. Autumn frosts had turned the trees along the river to blazing gold. Fat, sleek herds of Herefords grazed contentedly in the green meadows along the river benches. The rolling parklike hills lay warm to the sun under blue, Indian summer skies.

Great flights of Canada geese, and swift-winged flocks of migratory ducks flew up and down the river. At night the coyotes called under clear moonlight from the coulee rim. At dawn herds of mule deer fed at the forest edge. And all

day long cock pheasants crowed from the fields of yellow
grain ready to harvest.

There was a large crew of men already at the site when
we moved into the big old rambling ranch house. The bunk-
houses were bulging with men skilled in various trades. There
were cowboys and ranchhands for managing our herds of
cattle. A crew of cat-skinners had moved in to clear over
1000 acres of virgin terrain with their huge caterpillar equipment. Another gang was starting to build dams, dig irrigation ditches and excavate foundations for future plant
expansion.

There was a tremendous air of excitement and eager enthusiasm for the enterprise. As the fall season gently began to
give way to winter we became integrated into a highly efficient
team with excellent morale and stirring spirit of good will.
We were a part of that remarkable frontier world for which
the West has always been famous.

And, though I was a comparatively young man, those under
my supervision responded to my leadership with tremendous
loyalty and energetic work.

In our home, however, things were not quite as pleasant
as they appeared outside. The rambling old home was poorly
heated. Mother, who now lived with us, suffered from the
northern cold after her long years in the tropics. And Phyllis,
now carrying our first child, expected delivery about Christmas.

What disturbed the tenor of our personal lives more than
anything else was the unbelievable change mother saw in
my make-up as a man. We had not seen each other for many
years and my metamorphosis in the meantime came to her
as a traumatic shock.

No longer was I the rather quiet, shy, reserved lad who
had left Kenya with some apprehension in his heart. The
tough years of knocking about North America working with
all kinds of rough men on tough jobs had turned me into
a hard-headed, hard-driving, steel-willed individual.

In my youthful arrogance I considered myself to be a self-
made man. After all, I argued, I had come to the West with
nothing except a will to win. And I had won. Nor would I
allow anyone or anything to stand in my way to achieve whatever I wished . . . no one dared dictate to me!

Mother, who had unusual spiritual insight, sensed and

knew that, though outwardly my career was like a comet blazing across the sky with success, inwardly I was becoming empty, impoverished for lack of genuine personal communion with Christ. I was going great guns in the world of commerce. I was going nowhere with God.

Occasionally she would try to speak to me in earnest. But I was too busy breaking horses, riding the range, rounding up cattle, clearing land, laying out irrigation lines or supervising work crews to pay much attention. I was high in the saddle as far as the world went. But I was down in the dust of spiritual deterioration. I had no time now for church, for fellowship, for study of God's Word.

The ranch had become my "god." Work and performance had become a fetish. I was ready to lay down my very life to make my mark as a manager. Increasingly I became tougher, more forceful, and sinister as steel in my singlemindedness to succeed.

This caused both mother and Phyllis to grieve over the changes in my character and conduct. I often found mother in her room, kneeling before her rocker, weeping. She was crying out to God on behalf of her son. It seemed that in the twilight of her life sorrow was added to sorrow. And in very large measure I was the chief cause of her heartache.

The one great respite at the ranch was the birth of Lynn. Her arrival provided a new focus for the outpouring of feminine love so eternally essential to a woman's fulfillment. So the little mite in her basket by the huge, old, black, wood-fired stove in the kitchen was doted on by both mother and grandmother.

It turned out to be a ferocious winter. The river froze over solid. The ranch roads were cut off by huge drifts of snow. Brutal blizzards blew in from the north making a white hell for the herds of cattle we were wintering. The plunging temperatures and ghastly storms brought most of our operations to a white standstill.

The top company executives in their comfortable, plush offices at the coast, 300 miles away, fumed and fretted. They knew little or nothing of the horrendous hardships we were facing on the ranch. In typical corporation style they began to send out memos and directives as to what should be done on the site. As if they knew!

This galled me no end. As lucrative as my salary was, as

assured as my future might seem, as pleasant as the prospects for the operation appeared, I simply was not a man to be brow-beaten or pushed around by my employers. By spring break-up I, too, was ready to break out of the business.

As soon as our roads were opened to the outside world, I loaded my little family in the car and drove to Victoria on Vancouver Island. It seemed impossible that there, by the sea, gardens were already ablaze with daffodils, tulips and hyacinths, while the ranch lay buried under snow and ice.

In short order I found a lovely home for mother overlooking the shimmering straits of Juan de Fuca. There she could putter in her flower garden, have young people come in to share her home, and perhaps find a small measure of peace for the few years still left to her.

While waiting for the ferry to take me back to the mainland, and the ranch, I decided to put in the time taking a little drive along the coast. Suddenly I felt the urge to turn down a narrow gravel road that I had never been on before. It ran out across a pleasant peninsula called Rocky Point. On either side sheep farms rolled down to the edge of the sea. It was beautiful, parklike countryside dotted with giant Garry oaks and stately stands of fir and hemlock trees. The green pastures were dotted with flocks of flourishing sheep, some already with lambs.

Suddenly the road just ended at the water's edge. An island lay offshore. Beyond the straits the snowfields of the Olympics sparkled in the spring sunshine.

I got out and took a short stroll around. The property along the road appeared neglected, well-nigh abandoned. Buried in some undergrowth I found an old real estate sign. The place was for sale! I delayed my departure a day and took Phyllis out to see the property next morning. We walked over the land carefully. Then Phyllis and I looked at each other. Our eyes spoke louder than any words. We had stumbled onto the place of our dreams. The search was over! We would make this our future!

We rushed back to the city and put a down payment on the land. A short time later I cut my company ties. We were on our own!

Fairwinds

We called this fine country property "Fairwinds." It was a name more fitting than we realized at time of purchase. For in looking back later in life I came to realize profoundly it was none other than the wondrous guidance of the wind of God's own Spirit that had led us there.

Despite my own determined drive to achieve my own ends, the Lord in His own gentle way was arranging the direction of my destiny. This, in part at least, was because of the potent prayers of my wife and mother, but also because deep down in my innermost being there was germinating a genuine desire, an inner longing, stirred by God's Spirit, to do His will in some rather remote and as yet unknown way.

"Fairwinds" was the sort of country estate which more than surpassed one's fondest dreams. Situated on the very southernmost tip of beautiful Vancouver Island it lay sloping softly to the south, overlooking the shining Straits of Juan de Fuca. It comprised 214 acres of prime land of so-called black prairie soil produced under native grassland graced with an open parklike Oak-Madronne association of trees.

It enjoyed magnificent seclusion with its location at the very end of the road and end of land. On two sides it was surrounded by the sea. It boasted over two miles of exquisite ocean frontage with eleven little gravel bays and coves carved out of the contorted, rugged, rock formations.

In every direction there were majestic mountain views. To

127

the east Mount Baker and the Cascade range of the mainland coast stood on the horizon. To the south and west the snow-clad peaks of the Olympics towered above the straits. To the north lay the rugged, rolling Sooke Hills where, in years to come, I would hunt deer and track cougar.

The land itself was bisected by a lovely winter stream. It fed a little lake near the ocean edge. Offshore a rocky island broke the force of winter storms. There small boats found safe anchorage in any weather—especially the tiny craft in which the local fishermen caught the shining salmon from the then prolific Pacific runs.

Grouse, pheasants and deer abounded on the wild and tangled acres, for in the long absence of a resident owner much of the acreage was reverting to bush. Flocks of ducks, geese and brant stopped here. It was a favorite resting spot on the Pacific flyway for all migratory birds.

Along the beaches there were excellent clam-digging and some oyster beds. All of this had attracted a scattering of squatters. So when we bought the property it was populated with a community of crusty characters who had built themselves rustic cabins at the water's edge from the boards, planks and cedar shakes cut from driftwood logs tossed up by the tides.

Being young, audacious and rather naive about the legal ramifications of so-called squatter's rights, I assumed rather naively that my erstwhile "neighbors" would just quietly "move off" when I "moved in." It was not that way. Some had lived there as long as twenty-seven years. It was home to them. They were loath to leave.

Fortunately for us one of the seaside shacks stood vacant. We immediately occupied it for our own use. I built a bunk of driftwood in one corner as a crib for our baby. It was only a two-room place, but Phyllis soon turned it into a cute and cozy cottage. She hung curtains at the windows, pictures on the wooden walls, and bright carpets on the rough floors built from driftwood planks.

The ranch itself, as a ranch, was really a shambles. In the absence of the American investor who had bought it for spec-ulation, then left it untouched for thirty years, it was rapidly reverting to a pristine state. It had been rented out for grazing . . . more aptly overgrazing. Too many sheep and cattle had done enormous damage to the natural vegetation. Native grasses had been supplanted by poverty grass. Erosion was rampant. Huge gullies were washed out by winter rains. Fences had rotted out and the whole place had the pathetic appearance of a ranch crying out for love, care and intelligent management.

I could clearly see and sense all of this. Beyond the abused pastures, beyond the broken fences, beyond the accumulated debris and rubbish scattered everywhere by the careless squatters I could envisage a magnificent seaside property, flourishing with quality livestock, resplendent in total restoration.

It was a stimulating challenge. Never, ever had anything in life so aroused my spirit or fired my enthusiasm. Finally I had found my dream place. My future was totally assured. Here I could at last put down roots forever. My family could grow up on these tranquil, sunwarmed acres by the sea in quiet serenity. For my children there would be no shunting about from place to place, no upheavals and overturnings such as I had endured all my youth.

"Fairwinds" was forever!

I had found my heaven on earth.

I exulted in it with enormous passion and unbridled pride.

As is almost invariably the rule in life, there were several "flies in the ointment" of our glowing excitement.

The first and foremost was the very basic question of survival financially. The previous owner had died, the estate had to be settled, and we were obliged to pay all cash for the land. Even though our initial offer was low and accepted by the executors it consumed almost all of our accumulated assets. In fact, by the time we had moved in, purchased a minimum of equipment, and planted our first crops we were barely solvent by only 54 cents.

This had placed me in a very strained position. At heart I was a cattle man. I loved good cattle. Now, strictly because of financial limitations, I was forced to go into sheep because I could not afford cattle.

For me sheep were rather foreign. I found them stupid, rather helpless, and in our area extremely vulnerable because of cougar attacks and poaching by rustlers. I was not at all keen about launching a sheep operation. But sheep it had to be if we were to survive the first few years. Eventually my aim was to replace them with high-class registered Shorthorn cattle.

My immediate neighbor had been born and lived his whole life on his fine ranch. He and his wife became very fond of us. Like an older brother he took a vital, personal interest in our progress. Patiently, skillfully, persistently he introduced me into all the intricacies of sheep husbandry. A sure and fine foundation had been laid in this field for me by dear old George Brown back at the research station. But now it had to be built on by learning all the art of breeding, feeding, shearing, lambing, folding, butchering, docking and a dozen other essentials that spell the difference between a mere "sheep owner" and a master "sheepman" or shepherd.

It was not an easy transition from cattle to sheep.

And for the first years I actually resented deeply being stuck with such insecure creatures. In fact, in my moments of frustration with that first small flock I would burst out in vehement shouting, "Why in the world must I be stuck with such stupid knotheads!"

It was a classic example of how little we are aware, at times, that our Father's hand is upon us for good amid all of our apparent confusion and turmoil.

The first crop of lambs that came off the place were born amid ferocious spring storms. Sleet and snow and bone-chilling rain sweeping in off the straits raised havoc with the ewes and lambs. I would go out hour after hour into the terrible weather to gather up chilled, frozen lambs. In grim, black anger I would shake my fists at the sky and shout angry imprecations against the God of heaven.

If He really cared about us why did we have to suffer so? Why didn't He give us better weather?

Looking back now I tremble at my angry audacity against my heavenly Father. Yet in the same moment I marvel at His own remarkable forbearance and patience with one so petulant and perverse.

Perhaps in His own winsome way, my heavenly Father was smiling whimsically to Himself. For it was in the furnace of my own fierce frustration with that flock I was being given a vivid insight into the Good Shepherd's frustration with me as a man. Some of us can only learn the profound principles of divine life through the painful, breaking events of practical experience in our own walk with God.

Many of the truths shared subsequently with readers the world around in my books, were learned in the loneliness and agony of those first grim years at "Fairwinds."

Fortunately for me, for my family, for the flock, and for the ranch I learned rather rapidly how to handle sheep. Combining this skill with my expertise in land management, the entire operation quickly began to respond to the love, care and attention given to it.

In just a couple of years the entire complexion of the property was transformed. I worked like a man driven by an inner dynamo. Old fences were torn out and replaced with new ones. A fine gravel road was built leading to the cottage. The fields and meadows became lush and green with new growth. I cleared out the overgrown acreage, sparing choice specimen trees so that the entire estate took on the appearance of a beautiful English park. A new concrete dam and spillway were put in to enlarge the lake. We had a magnificent big vegetable and fruit garden, irrigated all summer, with such a surplus we could share produce with our squatter neighbors.

It was these latter people who were the other "fly in our ointment." Under Canadian laws of the land, squatters cannot be evicted. So it seemed we might be stuck with them, their shacks and their refuse forever.

It was here that I learned an enormous lesson in Christlike behavior from Phyllis. In her quiet, serene, gentle manner she said to me, "Phillip, tough tactics will never move these people. Only love will. Let us try and see their standpoint."

So we befriended them all. We lived at their level. We shared our surplus fruit and vegetables with them. I hauled them back and forth to town, twenty-five miles away, in my battered old truck. Phyllis shared cookies and cakes and favorite recipes with them. We invited the eldest into our home to share meals. I went over and split wood for the feeble ones. We carried mail and medicine and groceries for those too indigent to get their own.

One dawn I was awakened by the sound of someone hammering furiously on some cedar logs floating in the bay outside our windows. One of the squatters was building a float.

He winched his cabin off the beach onto the log boom and within twenty-four hours towed it away. It was the beginning of a mass exodus. Within a few months of that memorable morning, all eighteen families who had occupied the ocean-front moved away to live elsewhere.

We were left in magnificent seclusion to clean up the litter they had left behind, turning our tideline into one of the most exquisite waterfronts in all of the Northwest.

The tide had also begun to turn in our financial affairs. I had taken a part-time job working in a nearby lumber mill. As I used the proceeds to purchase more stock, equipment and ranch supplies, the entire operation gathered increasing momentum.

With titanic enthusiasm we demolished and disposed of all the old debris left behind by the squatters. Well over twenty tons of rusting engines, stoves, beds and broken metal were hauled away by scrap dealers. Tons and tons of old clothing, decaying furniture and junk were buried in eroded gullies. The entire place began to sparkle, shine and sing beneath the whispering winds off the ocean. Several cabins were left behind vacant. These we refurbished, painted and refurnished. Soon they were being rented out to summer guests, some of whom came from as far away as New York and Boston.

One day a magnificent car parked at the end of the road, outside our gate. I was busy spreading a load of gravel on our driveway, dressed in rough denims and bush jacket. The owner got out and walked up and down the fence gingerly, then hesitantly pushed open the gate and came in.

"Where's the owner of this estate?" he inquired, peering at me through his heavy horn-rimmed glasses.

"I am," I replied with a grin, my shovel held hard in my strong, calloused hands.

The stranger gasped in utter disbelief. "You are?" A long pause. "You have turned this property into an absolute para-dise!"—"Where are all the squatters?"

It turned out he was one of the wealthiest men in all Canada. For sixteen years he had been considering the purchase of the property, but his lawyers had advised him against it, since they could not shift the squatters.

He was an American, who had been one of President Roosevelt's top financial advisors. Now he was standing before me aghast at what love could do.

He came into our humble cottage and shared a cup of steaming, fragrant coffee and home-baked scones. From that day a fine friendship was forged between us. Subsequently I was to become his private land consultant. He owned immense holdings of property all over the country. My responsibility was to suggest the most efficient manner in which they could be brought into maximum production.

In ever widening ways the wondrous wind of God's Spirit was moving in my life. Yet at times I was too dull, too obtuse to detect His direction at all.

Joyous Years

As THE RANCH RESPONDED to my labor and my love it became an estate of winsome attractiveness. Its rolling meadows, lying warm to the sun on a southerly slope, were becoming increasingly lush, green and ever more productive.

A highly specialized system of intense sheep management, first developed in New Zealand, was initiated. I acquired the finest championship rams that could be bought to sire my lambs. Only the sturdiest, strongest high-quality ewes were used for breeding stock.

The net result was that with the combination of skilled land management and expert sheep husbandry I soon owned a highly productive livestock operation. Some years there were so many twins and triplets that a 180 percent crop of lambs were raised successfully.

There was a splendid market for local lambs in the city of Victoria, and it did not take long to develop a strong demand for the top quality produce from "Fairwinds." The wool crop was shipped away to the woolen mills in Winnipeg and Toronto for manufacture into handsome shirts, suits and world-famous Hudson Bay blankets.

Besides the livestock returns, I had diversified our operation by selling truckloads of Christmas trees and choice Alder cordwood to the wealthy homeowners in the city. They were pleased to have direct delivery to their doors and paid handsomely for such personal service and care. At the same time the returns covered the costs of clearing more and more acreage of beautiful parklike property.

All kinds of people began to hear about "Fairwinds." So they would drive out from the city to see the place. Shyly they would request permission to stroll quietly along the lovely shoreline, to wander across its peaceful pastures. We were glad to share our joy.

Our seaside cottages quickly acquired a reputation as a tranquil retreat where couples could come and enjoy a holiday in serene seclusion by the ocean edge. I even bought a boat and rented it out to those who enjoyed the splendid salmon fishing at our "front door."

The difficult, drab days of financial struggle were now behind. The income from our work and expertise increased dramatically. We had taken an abused and beaten piece of ground and with tender care and enormous energy turned it into a flourishing enterprise.

There was a sweet sense of artistic achievement in all of this. In a wondrous way we had worked in harmony with the earth and she had rewarded us in lavish abundance. It was a stirring sensation of rich success coupled with joyous achievement.

Often the famous words of Swift came to my mind: "Methinks, he who makes two blades of grass to grow, where only one stood before, does greater service to his country than either politician in parliament or preacher in pulpit."

Actually this was a profound part of my problem in a spiritual sense. I had come to love my land with such intensity, to revel so fiercely in the natural beauty of our sea and mountain world, to rejoice so exultantly in my home and family that the interests of God were now relegated to secondary importance.

It was not that we neglected the church, the Word of God, or our daily devotions. We did not. Quite the contrary. Like other millions of modern-day Christians, we went through the regular routine of religious rituals, but they were dry as the dust in my sheep corrals, and just about as barren.

Almost by default I concluded subconsciously that my joy in life could come from the earth and need not come from Christ.

Yet the strange irony of my inner spiritual stagnation was

that deep down within my spirit there was an intense hunger to really know God. There persisted an insatiable thirst to commune with Christ. But how?

Sunday after Sunday we would drive twenty-five miles to church. I would come with intense longing for some fresh spiritual inspiration or insight. But there was little or none. I had heard the same old phrases, the usual clichés, the pat platitudes so often I could quote them verbatim without even thinking. I almost knew by rote the next sentence the minister would say in his prayer or quote in his sermon.

Like a young ram which had come to a stall hungry, eager to be fed, then finding only dust, I would turn away to leave frustrated and raging with fury. Again and again I said to Phyllis, "I'm so fed up with the church and its chaff I'll never darken the door again." It all seemed so empty, so hollow, so hopeless.

Then one Sunday, when an unusual winter storm had us blocked in with blinding blizzards I turned on the radio. The voice I heard was a Methodist minister from Washington. Immediately all my senses were alerted. He spoke of spiritual issues in simple parables, much like Christ did, and in a manner I could quickly grasp and understand. His homely topics were such things as "High Tide," "Above Timberline" and "The Wind of God's Spirit."

It was a turning point in my walk with God. I began to have an awakened and renewed interest in things spiritual. Nothing, absolutely nothing on the ranch could keep me from tuning to that one-hour broadcast. Lambing, shearing, haying, land clearing, were all set aside to drink in those few moments of life-giving lectures.

The minister and I began to correspond. Eventually he came all the way out to visit us on the ranch. God in His mercy had sent me His messenger when I so desperately needed direction.

His friendship, his encouragement, his counsel added a new and widening dimension of joy to our days on the ranch. He introduced me to some of the best books among the Christian classics. My soul and spirit drank deeply from them. All of this was an exciting stimulus to my own creative urge to write.

Even though I worked tremendously hard on the land,

and end of day would find me exhausted, after supper and a relaxing hour or two with my family, I would pick up the pen and write diligently until almost midnight. Year after year I wrote and wrote and wrote. Nothing would ever deflect me from my determination to become an author of international stature. I would succeed!

Essays, articles, manuscripts and poems written in our humble cottage were sent off to editors, publishers and periodicals all over Canada and the United States. Again and again the letters of commingled rejection and encouragement came back. It was fine writing—*but.* I learned early that one had to have the hide of a rhino and the tough constitution of a camel to survive and finally succeed in this tough field.

But I refused to be beaten. So I kept at it.

Meanwhile about this time our second child was born—a boy—Rod. Phyllis and I were delighted. We had originally planned to have four children. But it became apparent two would be sufficient. This was not because of selfish reasons, but simply because it was obvious Phyllis was not physically strong enough to care for a large family. We were so glad Lynn in her tender years found genuine joy in helping around our humble home.

Both youngsters thrived in our exciting realm of natural beauty and expansive outdoor activities. The ocean, the hills, the beaches, the birds, the forests and fields, the sheep and crops all contributed to a pattern of joyous, carefree contentment few children ever experience or relish.

One of their various delights was our magnificent border collie, Lassie. When we first came to "Fairwinds" I owned a splendid big cattle dog. But he had no idea how to handle sheep. So a substitute had to be found.

I noticed an advertisement for a registered sheep dog in the local paper. When I went to see the animal I found it hobbled from leg to neck by a chain, in a vain attempt to break it from chasing boys and bicycles in the town.

The handsome, intelligent creature was already two years of age, yet had been taught nothing—not even the command, "Come." I decided to take the dog on six-weeks' trial. If in that time it could not be trained at all, it would be returned to the owner to be destroyed.

Though I had prepared a new kennel for Lassie, and we

laid out fresh water and food for her, she refused to touch anything I offered her. Day followed day this way. Finally I decided to loose her. In a rush she disappeared into the woods. I thought she was gone forever.

Several days later I saw her crouched on a rock outcrop watching me. So I placed food and drink for her there. Then she began to watch me at a distance as I handled the sheep. But at my call she fled. Week followed week in what seemed frustration.

Then one evening just at sunset as I stood alone with the sheep I felt a warm nose touch my hand from behind. She had come on her own! My heart raced with joy.

From that first faltering contact Lassie went on to learn to love and trust me completely as her master. She had an enormous, instinctive desire to please me, to handle my sheep and to be my joyous co-worker.

In a few months she learned all the necessary vocal commands. Then she progressed to working by hand signals. In time she became so remarkable in handling sheep that strangers would come all the way from the city just for the pleasure of watching her work with me in managing my stock.

From my constant intimate association both with this beautiful dog and my flourishing flock I was being given powerful insights into my own relationship to Christ, my Master. For the first time many of the majestic passages in God's Word which reveal to us our human role as that of sheep in the Good Shepherd's care began to carry positive impact for me as a man.

Profound questions which previously puzzled me in God's dealings with us as His people began to be understood. In the practical day-to-day operation of the ranch I began to see ever more clearly, in a spiritual sense, what my Master was trying to do with me.

Some of those basic principles were many years later to be shared with other people all over the world. First it would be in simple lectures, then eventually in books, tapes and films that God in His wondrous way would use to enrich millions of lives.

It was the age-old principle of our Father's gentle, yet strong ability to take a small thing and turn it into a mighty force for good in the earth. One lone rancher; one small energetic collie; one flock of sheep on a rugged chunk of Canada's coast. Yet from such humble things bountiful blessings would be brought to men and women around the world.

By now I was a man of thirty. Many of my most cherished hopes and dreams had come into vibrant reality. I held clear title to one of the most desirable properties on the west coast. I delighted in my lovely wife and family. Our home was a haven of joy and deep delight. My income was escalating steadily every year. In fact, I began to lay plans to buy out my neighbor's holdings and double the size of my operation. We had an ever-widening circle of fond friends.

It seemed our future was totally assured. Every joy and hope I ever held for my family's contentment was vested in this lovely piece of productive land by the sea. My self-assured confidence knew no bounds. I would just keep on building ever bigger and better ambitions.

In all of this adventure, amid this increasing affluence, surrounded by such seeming security and success, my faith and confidence had been, not in God—but in my own ability to get a job done. It is true I did begin to recognize that God's hand moved behind the scenes of my affairs. But like millions upon millions of other nominal Christians I carried out my own plans, my own program, my own purposes, for Phillip Keller.

As if to compound my conceit, I then had the double audacity to beseech God to come and bless all I did. The effrontery of such behavior never occurred to me then. Now I tremble at my own temerity. I marvel at the magnanimous patience and gracious longsuffering of my heavenly Father. I am broken as I contemplate His patience and kindness with one so proud and perverse.

My godly father-in-law, helping me clear land one frosty winter morning, put it to me humorously but honestly with a soul-shaking remark. "Phillip—you're so full of yourself and your own interests you cannot possibly be filled with the Spirit of God."

If I had any faith in those days, that faith was in my own skills, initiative, hard work and formidable determination to do well in whatever I tackled.

Even outside my own immediate work I had found ways to influence others. I prevailed upon the Federal wildlife authorities to declare our area a bird and wildlife sanctuary for the migratory species that passed through or wintered in our protected bays. The birds came in their thousands. The guns were silenced, and the flocks found respite from shot and shell within full view of our shining cottage windows.

All of this was tremendously gratifying, stimulating, exciting. The whole field of resource conservation fascinated me. Little did I then know how soon I would be thrust into the struggle for environmental concerns on an international scale.

At this point in time, like the wild flocks filling our sunset skies in full flight, everything in life just seemed so peaceful, so pleasant and ever so promising.

Shattered

ABOUT THIS TIME in my career, one of my former colleagues from the company with whom I had worked on seed production came to visit "Fairwinds." He was a crusty, brilliant soil scientist, then considered the finest in all of Canada.

He was an avowed atheist and had often taunted me for my Christian convictions which he considered archaic. But as he walked over the beautiful property by the sea, it was obvious he was deeply impressed by its unusual attributes.

He later wrote me a most moving letter, part of which I have never forgotten: "Phillip, you are the only man I ever met with courage enough to part ways with the company. More than that, you have found one of the most unique places on the whole planet to spend your days, your skill, your strength. Your future is absolutely assured!"

His sentiments were an exact echo of my own outlook.

At "Fairwinds" we were favored with the finest climate to be found in all of Canada. Located at the southern extremity of Vancouver Island, surrounded by the sea, it was not unusual to have gardens bursting with tulips, daffodils, narcissi and hyacinths in January. . . while the rest of the nation was locked in snow and ice. We enjoyed more hours of bright sunshine all year than any other spot in the whole of British Columbia. It was a bit of paradise.

One of the aged squatters who had occupied a shack on the beach actually came there to die. Doctors had given him only six months to live. But the balmy weather, the fresh sea air, the tranquil life of a fisherman had restored his strength. When we came his life expectancy of less than six months had stretched out to seventeen years.

Much the same had happened to me. From childhood my body had been racked with tropical dysentery, malaria and other debilitating diseases. Often friends and well-meaning associates had urged me to undergo extensive medical treatment. But I preferred to just push on in spite of recurring attacks of illness that sometimes left me very near death. Phyllis was often alarmed by the violence of my recurring malaria.

At "Fairwinds" all of this began to change. With our vigorous outdoor life style, heavy manual labor, abundant sunshine and joyous home my health improved steadily. My body built up with strong muscles of enormous resilience. I began to experience a level of energetic vigor that met every challenge with enthusiasm.

Each week when we went into Victoria for supplies, I would spend an hour or two swimming and diving in the gorgeous Crystal Gardens attached to the world renowned Empress Hotel. There I met some of the top Olympic athletes who were swimming enthusiasts. They coached me in both swimming and high diving so that these became an exhilarating athletic pursuit.

In the city we also had access to all the amenities provided by the Provincial government in its august Parliament buildings. My insatiable thirst for fine literature and good books was steadily satisfied by the magnificent Provincial library. I became close friends with the Provincial Museum curator and his fine staff of biologists and naturalists. All of them visited us at "Fairwinds," widening and expanding my growing interests in the conservation cause.

Because of my own intimate contact with the whole natural realm of sea and land around us I became very familiar with a wide range of wildlife. This exciting field experience was augmented and stimulated by wide reading and intense study in ecological subjects. Very quickly I was becoming an ardent field naturalist. The diversity of birds, fish, plants, trees and varied terrain which surrounded us stimulated me. I learned to know and love them all.

In truth and in sincerity it must be said here that in my

early thirties I was a man intensely, fanatically in love with
life.

Few men ever loved a piece of land as I loved "Fairwinds."
Few men ever reveled in their environment of sea and shore
and shining mountains as I did.

Few men were ever so sure that everything they needed
for economic security and social success was assured.

It was all there at my doorstep for the taking.

If I wanted fresh venison, there were deer in the hills. If
we wanted a choice leg of lamb, there was my flock. If we
wanted a steaming bowl of clam chowder, I simply went to
the beach at low tide. If we preferred thick salmon steaks,
I gently slipped my boat into the tide and took a spring or
coho from the clear waters.

Our table was laden with the finest of fresh fruit and home-
grown vegetables. There was always an overabundance. The
root-house shelves bulged with jars of preserves, barrels of
pickles, and crocks of salted herring.

Our home rang to the happy laughter of youngsters bursting with energy and health. We loved to sit around the open
fire and roast lamb chops or hot dogs or marshmallows. The
cottage windows were flooded with bright sunlight that
bounced in off the silver sea at our door. At night they were
awash with the mellow silver light of a magnificent moon.

Often I would go out into the silver light with Lassie. We
would wander along the shore, around the lake, up the
stream, across the meadows. I carried a rifle with me in case
of cougars on the prowl or rustlers on the road.

But the whole world of fields and forest, ocean and islands,
hills and mountains lay beautiful beyond words to describe.
I would stand still, silent, breathing deeply as if to inhale
and assimilate the mysterious wonder of it all.

Every dream I had ever cherished had come to life in this
lovely spot. Every hope I had ever clung to during the long
years of struggle to survive had been fulfilled here. Every
longing that lingered in my mind for self-sufficiency had been
satisfied here.

I felt as snug as a clam in its shell—before the shovel
strikes.

I felt as strong as a Blacktail buck in the prime of his
autumn glory—until the bullet strikes.

I felt as swift as the King salmon until the lure strikes.

Then it happened!

It was a gorgeous, warm spring day in mid May. The pastures were at their peak. The flock was lying in quiet contentment under the great spreading oaks. The skylarks were flinging their songs into the clear blue skies.

A big car drove into our yard. Out stepped two professional men in fine suits, brief cases under their arms. Immediately I recognized one as the tough, hard-headed real estate agent from whom I had bought the property. He was a retired Army colonel with a bristling mustache and brassy military bearing.

"Well, Keller, it's years since I saw you or this property," he remarked casually, glancing over the landscape. "I would hardly know it was the same place—you've made a showpiece out of it!"

I thanked him for his remarks, but wondered why he was there. I had never cared for his abrasive, arrogant personality.

"Would you consider selling?" he asked, twitching his mustache.

"No, definitely not!" I replied with vehemence. "Not at any price to anyone! I've found everything I ever wanted here! I'm set for the rest of my life!"

There was a long pause. A stern silence fell between us. Then with piercing eyes he looked at me rather belligerently and growled in low tones.

"Keller, you've got to sell. The Federal authorities in Ottawa are taking all of Rocky Point as a military arsenal for the Pacific fleet—" He hesitated a moment as if to savor his next sentence, "You've got to go!"

It was as if a high velocity .303 bullet had exploded within my brain.

I was shattered, as if struck with a blinding flash of flame and pain.

There was not even the mercy of shock to save my senses. Everything—everything—everything swirled through my emotions, my mind, my will, in a screaming crescendo of agony.

It was the end!

Almost in a stupor Phyllis and I stared at each other.

Both of us turned pale, our faces blanched with fear, our hearts throbbing with commingled terror and trauma.

Where would we turn now?

Where could we go?

What was left?

To compound our confusion, the two agents showed very little concern or sympathy for our plight. Their job in cold, calculating commercial terms was simply to get our land for the government at the lowest price possible.

My first reaction was to refuse to negotiate. In response the colonel in a typical military maneuver with which I was so familiar replied, "Either you accept our offer or the Navy bulldozers will be flattening your fields and fences within ten days."

When the car finally drove out of the yard both Phyllis and I fell into each other's arms—totally distraught, totally undone, well-nigh destroyed.

Suddenly it seemed the sun no longer shone in the sky. All was darkness—despair, dismay.

In anguish of spirit I went to walk alone across the fields and meadows I had learned to love so well. Though I was in the very prime of my manhood, hot, burning, scalding tears blurred my vision, trickled down across my sun-tanned cheeks, then fell to the ground upon which all my hopes had been built.

All my dream castles crashed down around me.

All my security was shattered, blown to bits by this ill wind of violent events.

All my roots put down in this place with such sweat and toil and intensity were torn from the soil that sustained them.

What I had loved I had lost!

It has been a most painful ordeal to recount here the agony of those days. I have endeavored to do so in utter integrity.

What I did not then realize fully at first, amid my darkness and despair, was that it is in the most forlorn and forbidding episodes of life that our Father is often the most near to us.

Blinded by our own burning tears, enveloped in the swirling mists of our own unsteady emotions, goaded and driven by our own vehement volitions, we can scarcely sense much less perceive the purposes of God in our pathos.

My mother, as a beautiful young bride in the bush of Tanzania, had been stripped of every human support that in her extremity she might turn and find her faith in God—not man. She had often told me of this, I had read it in her memoirs. But it had never been made real to me. Few of us learn much from the example of others.

Now I, too, was standing stripped—shattered—unsure, alone with my agony and my God.

From the utmost depths of my spirit there welled up, in anguish and desperation, an unspoken plea for God to reveal Himself to me in this hour of darkness.

Over the ensuing weeks and months that prayer was answered. Not in spectacular divine revelations as some might suppose or expect, but rather in a profound inner awareness that my dreams, hopes, aspirations had all been founded on a false premise. I began to see clearly that I was so conditioned by the culture of the contemporary business community that my confidence was grounded in ownership of property, scientific skills, and man-made decisions—not in Christ.

And, what I had been shown was that the gracious wind of God's Spirit could, if He so chose, demolish all such security in a single blast of His breath. Not that this was an "ill wind" of evil events, as I imagined, but rather the benevolent breeze of divine origin that was sent of God to change the entire course of my life.

My responsibility now was to trim the sails of my strong and stubborn will so as to move in harmony with His will for me. It would take at least another ten or fifteen years of exciting adventures before God would be given full control of my career or conduct . . . but I would be trying!

Meanwhile, back on the ranch, we found ourselves caught in the tiresome web of government red tape that always attends such transactions. Having served in the wartime civil service, I knew it would be months before we were paid out. I stubbornly refused to get off the land until we had full payment in hand.

Most of the other ranchers, much older than I, were in a position to sell off their stock and retire into town. Not I. So I attended all their sales, bought up their sheep and turned them back onto their owner's abandoned pastures. The upshot was I had huge flocks of sheep roaming over several thousand acres of land while I waited for the "feds" to act.

The bulldozers did not come for nearly eighteen months. During that time we lived in magnificent isolation, cut off by armed guards at a gate across the road.

In a peculiar twist of irony the government was glad to have me there—glad to have my stock grazing down the grass—glad to be relieved of an otherwise serious fire hazard.

The income derived from the large number of sheep was a minor compensation for the loss of our land. And when in due course we finally were paid off in full I was, before the age of thirty-two, in such a strong financial position we could have retired in ease had we so chosen.

Even that, however, was no great consolation for our sadness. The price we received was in no way a true reflection of the real worth of that land. At current market values for property in that area, "Fairwinds" today, with its shining shoreline, would be worth well over twenty million dollars.

But God was beginning to shift my attention to other values of eternal consequence. It had taken a devastating event to achieve this. Still He had succeeded in beginning to redirect my interests from self-seeking to serving others. I began to look at life, the world, and all its ramifications in the new light of the absolute unpredictability of events. The only two sure things were "change" and *God.* All else was transient, temporary.

For the first time there began to emerge the feeble flicker of a faltering yet positive faith in our Father. A man had to put his trust somewhere. If not in property or his profession or people or the promise of so-called "real things," it would have to be in the One who never changes and who promises to be faithful and totally trustworthy to His followers.

I spent more and more time studying Christian classics. The writings of great men like Oswald Chambers, Henry Drummond, F. B. Meyer and David Livingstone began to make a profound impact on me. For life to be worth living it had to be lived in service for God and men—not just for self.

I began to take a fresh interest in missions, especially foreign missions. Their adventure, excitement and romance in service appealed to me. At least I felt it might be a way to put a shattered man back together again. Hope had not died completely in my heart.

A New Direction

DURING THE PROLONGED interlude in which we waited for the government to pay us off for our property, God permitted new influences to enter my thinking. For the first time in years, all the excitement, all the momentum, all the adventure of laying out fresh plans, then working out those plans, had come to a standstill.

It was as if a peculiar lull had enfolded us in quietness and relative stillness. It was actually God's arrangement for getting my attention in a way I had not given it to Him before. There came into my life people and experiences and fresh impulses of divine design. I say this, not to be pompous, but in gratitude to my loving Lord.

For though I was a man standing on the edge of an unknown, unsure future, rather shattered and shaken, He was there to redirect my paths.

The first sobering, soul-searching event was the discovery of cancer in Phyllis. In those days it was an even more ominous and dread disease than it is today. Though she underwent serious surgery to remove the malignancy it would remain a cloud that would cast its shadow over our lives for the next fifteen years.

When the specter of death stands grimly on the doorstep, it drives us to consider seriously the brevity of our days. We then begin to ask ourselves very serious questions: "Why am I here?" "What am I here for?" "Where do I go then?"

For answers I began to read the writings of God's great saints more urgently than ever before. In searching, intense ways I turned to the books of some of the most beloved Christian authors of the last two centuries. In so doing the strange irony was that I more or less bypassed what the Word of God itself had to say. In short, what men wrote interested me more than what God's Spirit had written.

With great earnestness I must state here the result was my chief preoccupation in life began to shift from one of self-interest and self-preoccupation to that of service for others. Not that this was not a desirable redirection, a good step, in my spiritual saga. The tragedy was that *it was not the best step.* It would take at least another ten or twelve years of tempestuous living in various parts of the world, in diverse adventures, before at long last I would stumble onto eternal truth that we are not here either just for self or just for service but for *the Savior . . . to know God and to love Him.*

Nothing less than God Himself, in all His wondrous plenitude, majesty and goodness can fully satisfy the searching, questing, longing spirit of man. Never, ever, until we come to know and love Him in intimate communion and accord, do we discover that quiet rest and inner contentment which is the true hallmark of the child of God whose priorities are in proper order.

In the meantime, as with thousands upon thousands of other well-meaning men and women, I would literally fling myself wholeheartedly into service for the Master. Somehow I felt sure that if I brought to bear the same enthusiasm, energy and drive there that I had expended for myself in the past I would find fulfillment in a new arena of life.

Previous to this, one late afternoon, a beautiful, gleaming boat, about the size of a regular salmon trawler, had slipped into our bay. We heard the rattle of the anchor chain, then watched from shore as two men, attired in rough woodsmen's clothes, climbed into their dinghy and rowed ashore to our cottage.

We could hear their hearty laughter, the snatches of songs and bits of humor as they grounded on our wave-washed gravel beach. It turned out they were a couple of Shantymen missionaries who visited remote ranchers, loggers, lighthouse keepers and miners scattered up and down the wild west coast line of Vancouver Island.

It was the beginning of a remarkable friendship that has lasted down to this very day. The impact of their good will, the open-hearted generosity of their spirits, their obvious enjoyment in their work impressed me ever so deeply. If these men could find such obvious joy in service to others, then surely the same could be true for me.

What I had not yet learned was the cardinal principle that it was not their self-giving that was the secret; it was not the service that was the key; it was the life of the risen Savior indwelling them who made their work so special . . . that made their personal contact with me and my family so precious.

Twelve more years of tempestuous times would pass before I would be invited to do a major book on their magnificent work on the West Coast. *Splendor from the Sea* would in time become a Christian classic among missionary journals, but I had some severe spiritual struggles to endure before that ever happened.

Yet in the energy, the enthusiasm, the dynamic delight of these rugged, frontier missionary men I saw an example of joyous service that I wished to emulate. It became a contagion.

About this same time an inconspicuous little blue airmail letter from Kenya arrived in our country mail. I opened it rather casually. Its contents stunned and saddened me. I actually stood still, holding the wind-blown sheet of pale blue paper shivering in my sun-burned hands.

It came from an elderly couple, friends of my family, who had served among the Masai tribe of Kenya for well over thirty-five years. I knew them well. They had been in my home when I was a boy. They had literally poured out their lives as spilled water for the proud, wealthy, world-renowned Masai who grazed their great herds of cattle across the sweeping grasslands of Kenya and Tanzania.

Now the letter told of the elderly couples' waning strength, of their need to withdraw from the field, of the earnest search for some young people who would come to take up the tribal work. Would we be interested?

The response within my spirit was immediate.

The challenge came with remarkable force.

Only a few weeks before I had read the moving book, *Last Chance in Africa*. It had heightened my awareness of the enormous complexities facing the fragmented African colonies then determined to gain their independence. The transition from colonial status to sovereign states would be fraught with great peril and formidable problems.

The question posed then was, "Could white men with great vision and self-sacrifice be found who would dare to lay down their lives in order that African people might learn to stand on their own feet?"

The little blue letter, blowing in the sea breeze at "Fairwinds," was but another breath of air in the "Winds of Change" that were blowing all across Africa, and the world. And somehow deeply, soberly, urgently, I sensed myself being caught up and carried along in the gathering whirlwind of current events arranged by the Spirit of God.

With the proud tradition of my parents behind me, I could not stand back as a casual observer.

My extensive training and wide experience in land management, animal husbandry and livestock production were skills and scientific expertise to offer the Masai.

With my insatiable appetite for adventure, and intense interest in resource conservation, this was, without doubt, a fantastic field of service. Masailand was one of the last great wildlife areas of the earth.

With my natural love and affection for Africans, especially the nomadic tribes, it was natural my enthusiasm was aroused and stimulated. I would be glad to go, eager to serve, willing to pour myself out for these proud people of the plains.

I rushed back to the cottage to share the letter with Phyllis. In her calm serene way she replied softly: "If that's God's place for us, let's go!"

It was such a spontaneous, straightforward statement it surprised and exhilarated my whole being. Suddenly there was a new direction, a fresh vista to our lives. Things were opening up. The lull was behind us. We would soon be on the move again.

I shot off a letter of excited enthusiasm to Kenya, asking for direction in applying to our friends' mission board for service. Naïvely we assumed that being eager and available for immediate action we would be accepted gladly—the more so since no candidates had been found on the field to work among this unresponsive tribe.

The Masai, arrogant and aristocratic people that they were, had long held white people and their so-called "civilization" in contempt. They had rejected the baubles and bangles of our materialistic culture. They ignored and rejected our monetary system, preferring their own equations of wealth as measured in livestock and land. They had well-nigh refused to respond to missionary endeavors among them. Their simple reply to the Christian message in large measure had been, "That way is good for you! Our way is good for us!"

Because of such resistance there was little enthusiasm for work among these magnificent people. The mission society preferred to assign their personnel to more fruitful fields. So our elderly friends faced the formidable prospect of retiring from the Masai with no one to take up their lifetime labor of love.

They, too, were sure we would be welcomed wholeheartedly by the mission board.

It was to prove otherwise. Such is the ponderous and at times unwieldy machinery of mission and church organizations.

Phyllis and I filled out innumerable forms, tedious reports that divulged endless details. I even flew all the way to Chicago and back at my own expense to meet in person with their candidate committee. But it was all to no avail. They simply would not have us.

Unlike our heavenly Father, whose only single requisite for service is our availability to His purpose, human societies demand endless qualifications. Modern mission boards insist on special training, educational degrees, sophisticated techniques and complicated financial guarantees of support before a candiate is considered fit for the field.

For Phyllis and me it came as a traumatic turndown to be told that because neither of us were Bible school graduates, we were really not suitable missionary material. Besides this, we had young children who were considered to be a handicap for anyone living in very remote areas. And of course, because both of us had suffered from debilitating diseases, like malaria, cancer, dysentery, and so on, we simply were not fit for the Masai work.

This was the second time I had stood ready to return to Africa to do whatever needed to be done. Both times my offers to go had been rebuffed by men in the higher echelon of mission boards. I was determined they would not stand in my way again.

I would go anyway! I would go on my own just as my father and mother had done! I would go in the quiet confidence that if God could do great things for them, He could likewise open opportunities for me!

For the first time I was beginning to take steps of firm faith in our Father. It thrilled me no end.

I believe at the time some of our friends, and even family members, felt our decisions were dangerous and well-nigh foolhardy. It is always that way when a man or woman steps out to serve God in total abandonment to His purposes.

The terrorists of the Mau Mau movement in Kenya had launched their attacks against the church and Christians. They had turned against the government and all white people.

Death, bloodshed, and terrible fear gripped the country. Native Christians were burned to death in their huts. Terrorist gangs slaughtered white settlers and officials on their farms and stations. Bloody orgies were carried on in the forests and bush hideouts.

Surely no one in his right mind would take his wife and two children into such terrifying territory. It was utter madness!

But for us there was no fear— no foreboding—no faltering.

We felt the Wind of the Spirit of God pressing upon us. He had work for us to do clear across the earth. He it was who would lead us, protect us, provide for us in wondrous ways beyond our wildest dreams.

But before any of that could happen we had to get there. In swift, sure strokes I advertised the sale of all my sheep, ranch equipment and our household effects. Within a few days, in marvelous ways, everything was sold.

Taking the proceeds, I booked passage to Great Britain, then down to Capetown and finally up to Mombasa. All expenses were paid for out of our own pockets. After an absence of fourteen years we would celebrate my thirty-second birthday back on the warm, sun-drenched soil of the land of my birth.

Only one thing remained—Lassie.

In anguish of heart I took her for a last lingering walk along our beloved beaches. There, on a rocky knoll overlooking the ocean we loved, I put her to rest. It was one of the hardest things I ever did. The end of an era had come for both of us.

Momentarily I looked back across those tempestuous, rugged years of tragedy and triumph. Everywhere there remained the indelible impress left by the wonder of God's own gracious Wind at work upon my life. Always, ever He had been there present and active behind the scenes. His patience and His perseverance had prevailed. He had brought me from darkness to light, from despair to the joy of His own strong Spirit.

Part III

The Adventure Years

Africa Again

A PRESSING SENSE OF URGENCY, combined with exquisite excitement enfolded us as a family in the days before our departure. For me as a man it was a case of "going home" after so long an absence. For my wife and children it was to face a new frontier. For mother, now in very frail health, it was the answer to her years of prayer and anguish of spirit on my behalf.

Her son, at long last, was flinging himself unflinchingly into the Master's service. She could ask no higher honor. In the twilight of her times this was the glory of the afterglow granted her by her Father before her call "home."

Bravely, buoyantly she bade us farewell. She shed tears, not of self-pity for the loneliness she would endure to the end of her days, but tears of triumph, for at last she had lived to see God's will at work in my life . . . to a degree.

Her prayers, her flaming faith, her constant compassion would be honored by God to preserve us amid perils and dangers beyond our imagination. It is a fortunate person whose life and work is safeguarded by the outpouring of some unseen, unsung soul behind the scenes.

I wish to state here without hesitation, that in this respect, my heavenly Father has favored me uniquely. Beginning with my own parents and early, godly teachers, down to this very day, He has chosen in His own magnanimous way to provide faithful friends who intercede for me daily, who trust Him for my direction and protection, who participate in my ongoing adventures with Him by their love, their interest and selfless giving.

To be so honored is to be humbled.

Nor would it be appropriate to claim any personal credit for the achievements of later years without due respect to my praying friends. Some have been rough ranchers, brilliant scholars, retired missionaries and just plain people who truly love Christ.

I left several weeks before Phyllis and the two youngsters. There were essential engagements to meet across the continent. So I left by car. My family would fly to meet me in New York where we would board the majestic *Queen Elizabeth* for Britain.

First I stopped to spend a few days with my Mount Rainier friend. He had risen rapidly in the ranks of the U.S. Wildlife Service. Now he was superintendent of The Trumpeter Swan Wildlife Refuge in Red Rock Lakes, Montana. His field experience in wildlife observations, and fine photographic work on the native species of his mountain area, provided me with an excellent base for similar studies in Kenya.

It was like old times on the rugged ridges of Mount Rainier as we roamed across the magnificent Montana ranges. We were two intensely exhilarated young field naturalists. We shared stirring dreams of contributing to the newly emerging conservation cause, only just in its infancy.

We climbed the broken, gaunt ridges behind his big log house in quest of the cunning Bighorn sheep. We crawled through the tall marsh grass to stalk and photograph the majestic Shiras moose in their rutting regalia. We swept across the marshes in his air boat studying the regal Trumpeter swans in their sun-kissed sanctuary.

All of this was tremendously stimulating. Lying amid the tall tulles which had been turned to gold by early frosts, I decided I, too, wanted to record and study the wildlife of Masailand as my friend had done in Montana—with one difference. My camera equipment would have to be very light, very compact, very rugged to stand rough abuse in the African bush.

My next stop was to be with a dear fellow in Ohio who years before had first given me a small camera and taught me how to handle it. Now I needed his expertise in selecting a more advanced instrument that would serve me well for many years.

After long discussions and careful study we concluded that a Leica 35 mm camera would be the best investment. At that time Leica was recognized as the world leader in the photographic field. With the sturdy construction and meticulous precision so typical of German industry, Leitz had produced cameras of amazing accuracy and remarkable toughness.

It proved to be a most astute choice, for that camera and its lenses have been carried to more than forty countries around the world. Over a span of thirty years it has never failed to produce fine photographs. Its 35 mm slides have appeared in all sorts of magazines, journals, calendars and lectures, besides illustrating all my outdoor books.

It is an instrument that has been dropped by accident out of the top of an acacia thorn tree while photographing elephants. It has tumbled down a huge crevasse in a glacier in the Canadian Rockies. It has been bounced about my body in hundreds of rugged escapades. Still it functions flawlessly.

That same friend who guided me so skillfully in this choice, cared enough to travel down to New York and bid us all farewell at the docks. A dear, dear fellow! Last week he spent five special days in our home—still serene, still sweet in spirit, at the advanced age of 75.

My next stop was the Chrysler corporation in Detroit. In a generous gesture of good will they had agreed to sell me a Plymouth station wagon at cost, for use in Kenya. At their special invitation I was able to tour the production plant, meet with their executive personnel for overseas sales, and arrange to have the vehicle shipped to Mombasa at minimum expense.

This was an enormous encouragement. It was a firm, vital confirmation that our quiet faith in our Father's care was being vindicated. Here were total strangers extending practical, essential assistance to us in such generous measure. When I shared the good news with my family in New York, we all just hugged each other in happy gratitude and cheerful excitement.

Now we were ready, eager to leave.

This time there was no tug at my heart to return to the fading coastline. There was no anguish of spirit at sailing away into the unknown—no dark doubts about what might lie ahead.

Somehow in a serene assurance of moving strongly, surely in the purposes of God, we crossed the Atlantic with calm confidence. We were carried along in the powerful thrust of our Father's will, just as surely as this mighty greyhound of the North Atlantic surged ahead steadily under the tremendous thrust of her gigantic screws.

In London we boarded a brand new ship, *The Braemar Castle*, setting out on her maiden voyage around Africa. The gay bunting broken out to bedeck the ship, the stirring band music, the shining paint and sparkling metal made our voyage a special pleasure.

But at the island of St. Helena my spirit was strangely stilled. For I went to stand alone in solemn silence where Napoleon Bonaparte had spent the terrible, lonely twilight of his life. I had read and reread books about this passionate, proud man. What a life poured out in utter abandonment apart from the purposes of God! What enormous energies ending in disaster and defeat! What grandiose dreams turned to dust on this lonely rock in mid-Atlantic!

In quiet earnestness I bowed my head, humbled my heart. There, overlooking the great, gray, south Atlantic I besought God to deliver me from pride and arrogance that might lead to such utter human madness.

The ocean cruise was a special benefit to Phyllis and the children. It gave them a chance to mingle and chat with people who loved Africa, who lived there, who understood it. There was no sudden drastic culture shock that comes with flying in a few hours from one human society to another. Before long, bonds of friendship were forged with fellow passengers. So all of us were at ease, contented with new companions.

South Africa shook me!

I knew all about apartheid. We had discussed every detail of it during the weeks at sea. Books like *Cry the Beloved Country*, a classic by Alan Paton, had stirred my spirit to the very depths. I thought I was mentally prepared, yes, even emotionally ready to encounter this divided society.

But I was not.

My soul was torn, tortured and tormented by the cruel discrimination based only on the accident of birth and consequent color of a person's skin. I had lived that hell in high school.

That was thirty years ago. The anguish and agony still go on. How much longer the fabric of human frailty can endure such stresses remains unknown. In quiet moments of reflection one trembles to think what tremendous upheavals may yet occur in a land already drenched in human blood.

The rugged grandeur of Capetown's commanding situation on the Cape of Good Hope gave the lie to the hope crushed in the lives of its Bantu and Cape Coloreds. The lush orchards and world-renowned vineyards lying warm to the southern sun were but a mask worn by a land whose people lived with black animosity boiling in their veins. The lovely seaports of East London, Port Elizabeth and Durban with their golden beaches would one day tremble beneath bloody strikes and the terror of social eruptions.

Steadily our ship moved up the east coast of the giant continent. Few people realize the enormous expanses of the African bush. From Capetown to Nairobi is roughly 3000 miles, yet that is only half the distance to Cairo, still another 3000 miles beyond.

Finally we passed the mouth of the Zambezi River, and the coast of Mozambique. There flooded over me waves of mounting emotion as I recalled the incredible, remarkable exploits of David Livingstone in the interior of this region.

He had always been, and still is, one of my great heroes.

Seldom, if ever, had one man's life and work and mission made such a stunning impact upon an entire continent. Virtually alone, with irresistible courage he had crossed and recrossed the interior in his struggle to stop the diabolical slave trade that drained the very life of the region in brutal oppression.

Modern biographers have belittled Livingstone's utter self-sacrifice as a dedicated servant of God. They have done him great disservice. For ultimately it was his laid-down life that aroused the entire civilized world to the appalling devastation, horror and bloodshed perpetrated by the cruel Arab slave traders.

As a small lad I had sat in Matthew Wellington's humble

home and heard first-hand this simple African recount the exploits of his illustrious master. For it was Matthew and his several companions who secretly embalmed Livingstone's body and bore it safely out to this hot steamy coast. From there it was finally taken with great honor to be interred amid the solemn splendor of Westminster Abbey.

The world has ever deprecated the dedication of Christian missionaries. It despises their devotion. It brands them as misguided zealots. In reply one must ask in all seriousness: "Who else is bringing health, better housing, higher education, improved agriculture, new hope in Christ, freedom from slavery, and hope for the future?"

Certainly not the international business community, not the political opportunists, not the military establishment, not even the social do-gooders.

At last, after almost six weeks at sea, we dropped anchor in the quiet waters of Dar-es-Salaam—the Port of Peace. I could scarcely wait to slip ashore. For it was in this very spot, beneath the swaying palms, that my mother, as a beautiful bride of twenty-one, had first set foot on East Africa's soil exactly forty years before.

I walked along the sandy path softly as if in a trance. Fourteen long, tempestuous years had elapsed since I last inhaled the pungent perfume of Plumeria. The gentle cooing of the mourning doves drifted softly on the evening breeze. The whisper of the palms in the warm tropical air was music to a man so long away.

Then an aged African, attired in a flowing white kanzu (gown) and flowing white beard, approached me on the path. In the gentle accents of the coast he greeted me.

"Peace be to you, my friend. May God bless you!"

The familiar Swahili phrases, so well loved, so long dormant in my subconscious for so many, many moons, flooded back to my mind.

In an up-welling of good will, of excitement, of enthusiasm I poured out my emotions . . . my eyes brimming with tears of joy.

"My friend, I am back, back to the land of my birth, back to my brothers, back to the place of God's appointment for me—back to help heal the horror of Africa's heart."

An exquisite radiance covered his lined and weathered

countenance. A smile of total understanding lit up his face. He stetched out his hand, gnarled and worn with work, to rest it upon my arm.

"My son, I am so glad you have come home!" His eyes glowed warm with affection. "God has brought you back to us in our hour of need!" He hesitated a moment. "He will guide you surely in the paths of His choice." He pressed my arm gently, "Go in peace! All is well!"

The aged veteran turned and walked away.

Standing alone on the shore I knew of a certainty that I had met "the angel of the Lord" in common human guise.

He had conferred upon my spirit a blessing and benediction of sublime significance.

For me as a common man, this encounter was my special commissioning. Its impact never left me. I was back to do the bidding of my Master. In such assurance my spirit was quietly serene.

Among the Masai

A FEW DAYS LATER, in the broiling heat and intense humidity of Mombasa, we disembarked. It was in this very same spot that fourteen years before dad and I had said farewell for the last time. Now I had returned, bringing with me my wife, a daughter, a son and the sum total of all the vast experience packed into those years away. I had sailed from these shores a lanky lad. I came back a mature man.

We boarded the little, narrow-gauge train that ran inland to the great Lake Victoria. By night Phyllis and the young-sters, weary with the heat and endless miles of thorny nyika (scrub brush), fell asleep in their bunks. But for me there was no slumber. I sat wide awake at the window watching the Kenya landscape unfold under a brilliant equatorial moon.

Surging excitement swept through my being as gradually the bush country gave way to open savanna. Steadily, as the train gained the inland plateau, great open plains of bleached grass swept away to the hazy horizon. From long experience I could tell the country was dry, brittle, bleached as an old bone by months of sun and drought.

Here and there in the silver light of the moonlit night I could spot small bands of gazelles, wildebeestes and zebras on the plains. An occasional Masai manyatta (village) formed a darkened circle on the white expanse of the open landscape.

These were the people to whom I had come. This was the terrain to test a man's mettle in the months ahead.

"Oh, Father, here I am. This is the place of Your appointment for me. I trust You to prepare the Path before me." The thoughts unuttered in human syllables, still constituted a profound prayer of the utmost integrity. I had done my part in coming. God now would do His part in providing a place for us.

Our elderly friends who had written to us with such impassioned pleas to come, met us at the little wind-blown station on the Athi plains. Dear, sweet, sincere people, they took us to their humble home and without fanfare immersed us at once in an intense study of Masai lore and language.

"Masai" means the "wealthy ones" . . . wealthy in great sweeping grazing lands; wealthy in their proud tribal traditions as a fearless warrior race; wealthy in their huge herds of cattle and sheep; wealthy in their intense personal dignity as gracious individuals.

After lengthy consultations with our kind hosts, and after making several exploratory survey safaris it became obvious the need among the Masai was immensely more acute than anything I had ever imagined. Not only did they require spiritual redemption as a human society, but also scientific restoration from the ravages of land abuse that was turning much of their territory to desert wasteland.

In an act of bold faith, encouraged by our friends, I decided to drive into Nairobi to meet some of the senior British officials responsible for administering Masailand. In impassioned sincerity I explained why I had come back to Kenya. I shared with them my acute awareness of the enormous social, ecological and economic challenges confronting the Masai. More than that I expressed my willingness to be of whatever service I could in helping to heal such a fine and hearty people.

At first the official reaction was one of tempered restraint and caution, so characteristic of any civil service. However, in an action of respect for my sincerity they suggested I submit "a paper" to them, outlining concisely what I proposed to do among the Masai. At least they would be polite enough to consider my ideas.

This was all the more remarkable since the country was

caught up in the cruel crisis and awful atrocities of the Mau Mau uprising.

With great care and childlike prayer, trusting God's Spirit for every sentence we put on paper, Phyllis and I laid out a simple strategy. Step 1. Live among the Masai intimately. Become their friends. Learn all their social customs, traditions and intricacies of tribal behavior. Step 2. Make an exhaustive survey of their natural resources including grazing lands, vegetation, water supplies, livestock herds, wildlife populations and human nomadic practices. Step 3. On the basis of the foregoing gladly share with them the wondrous news of our Father's love in Christ. Suggest and outline practical, improved methods of land management, resource conservation and application of sound scientific technology in animal husbandry.

In a nutshell it was an exact replay of the superb work dad and mother had done several hundred miles away in another part of the country with different tribes.

To our utter astonishment a letter came back to us within ten days inviting me to meet with the top official in Nairobi. It was to prove one of the most poignant moments in all of my life up to that point.

Very briefly, emphatically and concisely I recall the hard core of his remarks to me in his office.

"Mr. Keller, we recognize your intense and intelligent concern for the Masai. We appreciate your coming in this hour of challenge for Kenya. Because the mission board will not have you as a member, we will give you official sanction to live among these people."

My heart began to pump hard with excitement.

"We happen to have an empty, brand-new bungalow, fully furnished, in the Kajiado district. We thought you would like to make that your home base. It is right among the Masai."

He twitched his dark mustache in deep thought. "And to satisfy the Masai, we feel it appropriate to appoint you as an extraordinary officer with a 'carte blanche' commission to carry out your studies. This will provide you with great freedom."

My eyes widened with commingled joy and elation. It hardly seemed possible.

"And to confirm to all concerned that this is in fact a bona fide arrangement, we are undertaking to pay you a full salary for the full term of your stay here."

I stood to my feet, gripped his hand hard, and held down the emotions which wanted to burst from the depths of my soul.

I don't remember driving back to my family and friends. It was more as though I floated there caught up and borne along on the updrafts of the wind of God's wondrous Spirit.

How faithful was our Father!

How totally trustworthy!

How sure! How reliable!

We had circled half the globe to reach this place, this hour, this appointment of God's arrangement.

He, in His turn, had prepared a people, a home, an opportunity for service, an income, an open-hearted acceptance with the authorities—all beyond our wildest dreams.

In gaiety and gladness we all flung ourselves into each others' arms. Tears of joy, tears of gratitude, tears of enormous hope tumbled down faces wreathed in wide smiles.

What a homecoming God gave us!

Step by step I was learning life with Christ could be a glad adventure, shot through with startling surprises, blood-tingling bonuses.

Within weeks the station wagon arrived from Detroit. Our few personal possessions were loaded, and we headed off into the "blue"—a local term for the African bush country.

The spacious bungalow, built of cut stone, sat on a commanding rise of land with wide vistas across unfenced plains, hills and dongas. Our only neighbors were the Masai manyattas near by. The closest white person was a lonely Scottish settler twenty-seven miles away.

We were on our own in the wilds! And it was wonderful!

Quickly we discovered that we were residing among a people of remarkable personal dignity, of unusual human decency and integrity. These sterling qualities of the Masai character generated enormous respect on my part for them as a tribe.

Our humble home quickly became a social center where for one reason or another they loved to come. The elders would drift up to the door, exchange elaborate greetings, then invite me to sit in the shade of a sweeping pepper tree while we exchanged news of our travels. Being a nomadic race they reveled in recounting the events of all their moves back and forth across the countryside.

They all loved and adored children with a moving intensity and heart-stirring sensitivity. Amongst the Masai there was never, ever, such a travesty as an "unwanted child" so common in our corrupt, crass culture. Every infant was a special, wondrous gift bestowed by the generosity of God. Children were a priceless heritage honored and loved by all. Because of this they just adored Lynn and Rod. Lynn's long, lustrous, finespun blond hair was stroked and caressed with awe and wonder.

At a very early age youngsters were entrusted with the care and protection of their siblings. The bonds of genuine brotherhood and sisterhood forged between families were beautiful to observe. The average westerner would be baffled by the intimate ties that enabled a youngster to call several men "father," or more than one woman "mother," because of profound affection one for the other.

Phyllis, who quickly endeared herself to the Masai because of her gracious, warm, shining spirit, marveled at their love. The married women, young mothers and laughing, happy teenage girls came every day for friendly family chats. In a simple, helpful way she tended their minor illnesses and accidents, but quickly discovered the Masai had excellent home remedies for many of their common complaints.

Just a few days after we arrived, a young lad, mauled by a lion, was brought to us. He had valiantly tried to drive off the predator when it attacked his father's stock he was herding. Though he speared the lion it turned and tore him savagely before succumbing.

Because the boy was in such dreadful agony, we laid him gently in the station wagon. Accompanied by his father and several uncles I rushed the thirty miles across the dirt track that crossed the open plains and put him in the care of a Hindu surgeon. He was quickly stitched up. Two weeks later he returned home in triumph, a young hero.

Between the Masai and us a remarkable, mutual relationship of trust and admiration developed. Very quickly they recognized with their acute perception that we were not there with any sinister self-interests or ulterior motives. And especially because of my own background of handling livestock they reveled in our common ground of intense love for the land and animals.

I would spend hours showing them photographs and pictures of champion livestock. Their utter astonishment was amusing. They would become so excited they would leap to their feet, cry out in ecstasy and shake their heads in total disbelief. They were amazed there could be bulls so huge, cows so productive or sheep so prolific in other lands.

This was doubly so, simply because their ancient and revered tradition was that when God created the earth, He entrusted to the Masai, and them alone, the care of all the cattle. So it was now their perfect right to lay claim to any livestock, anywhere. If need be they would take them by stealth or outright force.

This accounted for the huge raids made on neighbors' herds. Just a few months after our arrival, the Masai warriors in our district made a night attack on the Akamba tribe. In a twenty-four-hour period, they absconded with well over four thousand head. This would make the roughest Texas rustlers look tame.

Cattle comprised the center and circumference of their lives. Cattle were loved collectively, but also individually. Each beast bore a unique name, such as "The one calved at full moon." No matter how many head a man owned, they were each known by name. At evening and dawn, as the great herds entered or left the owner's gate, they were checked individually, never in massed numbers as we do in the west. All of this our Lord referred to in His parables.

Their livestock represented wealth, prestige, insurance against disaster, and social status. Above all else livestock comprised their chief food supply. On special festive occasions bullocks were butchered. Huge quantities of meat were consumed. And the blood was used either warm or congealed. Phyllis and I were invited warmly and happily to participate in all of these social events that took place to the accompaniment of much laughing, singing and merry-making. Though we never drank the blood, we relished their tough, roasted meat off the coals.

The staple diet at other times was milk. This was drunk

either fresh or clabbered. A Masai rule of thumb was that one should be able to consume a gourd of milk the size of one's thigh at a single sitting. I never was equal to this.

Because of their nomadic life style and contempt for manual labor in tilling the soil, they grew no crops. So on a spartan diet of milk, meat and blood they bore themselves in pride with magnificent physiques and incredible stamina.

In their culture there was no personal private possession of property or land. They held their countryside in common ownership. It always moved me deeply and touched my spirit afresh to hear them speak of "Our land. Our grass. Our springs. Our village." Like the early Christian church, reported to us by Luke in the Book of Acts, "they held all things in common."

In humility of heart I became increasingly conscious that God would use the Masai to teach me as much about dignified human behavior as I might ever be able to teach them about twentieth-century scientific technology.

The Conservation Cause

THE FIRST THREE MONTHS that I was back, over three thousand dusty miles were put in on safari over a greater part of the Masai reserve in Kenya and Tanganyika (Tanzania). What I saw then convinced me, more than ever, that if ever a country and a people needed a vision—a dream, a plan—it was Masailand.

Where in bygone days there had been rich, rolling grasslands, now there were hundreds of square miles of useless brush country with the gray tide of leleleshwe menacing new territory in its terrible advance. The green hills, where as a youngster on holidays I had hunted francolin and Guinea fowl, were scarred with hideous gullies of erosion that left them with great gashes of red and brown that floodwaters had cut.

Some of the finest water-courses like the Kimana, which used to flow clear beneath the lovely canopy of luxuriant trees that lined its banks, had degenerated to a muddy trickle that ate at the bare banks now shorn of trees.

Much of the beautiful, parklike country with its magnificent vegetation, which had been adorned with fine herds of game and native cattle, was degenerating into a pathetic wasteland. There remained the stark skeletons of burned trees, a few straggling wisps of dry grass, and numerous stunted thorn bushes as a reminder of a past glory. Instead of hundreds, or in some instances even thousands, of head of game, as in former times, they could now be counted in mere handfuls, scattered here and there.

Tragic as all this appeared, by far the most startling degeneration was in the people themselves and in their stock. Many of the young men and maids obviously lacked the physique, the mental alertness, the fine dignified bearing of their forefathers.

Little wonder, then, that my heart ached.

For hours at a stretch I would sit at the watering places and talk with the men who brought their cattle to drink— cattle so thin and poor that in one year of drought alone no less than 125,000 of them had dropped dead in their tracks out on the blasted plains. Their bones and carcasses littered the land in such profusion that even the hyenas and vultures could scarcely keep up with the orgy.

There at the water holes, or at the village gate, or in the shade of a sheltering thorn, we would talk of the past. The elders would swing their arms in great sweeping circles to encompass the distant horizon and mutter in hushed tones: "Once it was all white grass country." By that they meant it had been so rich with forage that the grass had grown tall, then in the hot sun turned to that bleached, pale shade so typical of the original African veld. But now, hands over their mouths in a token of despair, they shook their heads and stared blankly at the barren land punctured by short stubs of spiny grass.

What was happening to them was happening to much of Africa. It was the terrible tragedy of deserts on all sides extending their borders. It could be seen in South Africa, in Nigeria, in the Sudan.

All of the interrelated forces of overpopulation, overstocking, overgrazing, overburning were combining to reduce a once wonderful countryside into an uninhabitable waste—a place where neither man nor beast could survive.

The Masai themselves impressed me as being powerless to do much about it. Not that they would not have wished it otherwise—who wouldn't prefer to see their cattle sleek, their children strong? But in common with men of other civilizations who had declined from greatness, they simply shrugged their shoulders with an attitude of abject resignation: "The hand of fate."

The thing I found almost as disturbing about the situation was that this attitude was not confined to the Masai alone. One could detect the same frame of mind in conversation with governmental men, administrators, educators and others. It was as though "It just had to be."

Perhaps if I had not been a native son and known the country in some of its former glory, or if I had never been away from it to come back and be shocked by the awful changes that were taking place, I, too, might have been less outraged.

On the contrary, my heart burned. Something must be done. The insidious forces that were destroying Africa's wild glory must be halted. It became my obsession to see countermeasures set in motion that would preserve this magnificent land.

This, then, became my vision.

I could picture this splendid wilderness country garbed again in all its former glory. I could see it blanketed under a protective layer of rich vegetation that would absorb and retain the rains that fell upon it; that would cover the raw gullies and heal the scarred hillsides; that would shade and shelter the ghastly stretches of barren soil from the searing, cutting, drying ravages of sun, water and wind. Fertility would rise with increased humus; streams and rivers would run clear again; springs would flow through the long, dry months.

In this environment improved livestock and handsome herds of wild game would find an abundance of feed and water, more than ample to meet their needs and nourish their offspring.

The Masai people, awakening to their rich heritage, would husband it with the care and intelligence of inspired men— not only for themselves, but also for posterity.

If there was any better way to attempt the extension of the "kingdom of heaven on earth" I did not know of it.

With iron will I set to work to prepare the ground for this purpose. Uppermost in my mind was the determination to "know Masailand—and know it well." This alone would occupy most of the time and energy of the next few years.

What I did not then realize was that it was perfectly possible to become so caught up in a cause as to neglect Christ Himself whose cause it was. Or, to put it another way, as is so common among Christians engaged in God's work around the world, their service becomes of greater significance to them than the Savior Himself.

For the next few years I literally laid down my life in anguish of spirit and enormous empathy for the Masai. Their interests became my interests. Their losses were my losses. The destructive damage of the drought that ravaged their land put me through as much pain as theirs. Perhaps even more, for it was not just a case of losing livestock and facing famine, but the even more excruciating anguish of watching one of the earth's most magnificent grasslands deteriorate to desert wasteland.

For those who have been reared in an urban world, where the environment is largely man-manipulated, the agony of soul which I suffered in Masailand will have little or no meaning. This is not to act aloof or arrogant. Nor is it to be pretentious. It is simply a case of whether or not one has an intimate empathy for the earth; an understanding of the stresses to which the biota can be subject; an awareness of the destructive forces at work in the environment.

Those few of us who "see" the steady loss of good land; who "sense" with intense emotion the cruel ravages of human ignorance or greed on natural resources; who "plead" for the preservation of wilderness and irreplaceable native species, suffer in a dimension unknown to the majority of mankind.

This is not because of any special merit on our part. Rather, it is because of our intimate understanding of the earth's environment, and our special harmony with the natural world.

I am writing this chapter some thirty years from the time of my tears among the Masai. During that interim there has been a world-wide awakening to the rapid rate at which our natural resources are being ravaged and ruined. The voice of the so-called *Environmentalist* is heard in many places. In fact, it has become almost popular to stage protest marches or launch national publicity campaigns to arouse public opinion over environmental issues. A certain flamboyancy or fanfare often attends such demonstrations. But that is a far cry from the solitary soul at grips with the grim reality of combating human suffering in a setting where hunger, famine, drought, death and despair are the warp and woof of daily events.

For the first full year after our arrival, there was not a drop of rain in our area. The blue skies, sometimes graced with gorgeous cumulus clouds, burned with relentless heat. It had been that way for six months before we came. So for eighteen months the sweeping plains and hot hills shriveled in the sun. Everywhere I went the carcasses of livestock and game littered the landscape.

Gradually the grasslands were gnawed down to the ground. Roughly six million head of Masai cattle and four million head of wild game animals struggled to survive on the ever-shrinking vegetation. In places close to permanent water supplies the intense grazing pressure had finally wiped out the last vestiges of grass. In desperation sheep, goats, zebras and gazelles would dig up the dusty soil for a few shreds of roots that remained beneath the surface.

Streams turned to dry sun-drenched trenches of sand and rock. Springs faltered then failed. At best they might be a murky mud-hole tramped to soft clay by ten thousand hooves from the thirsty herds. Some Masai women trekked more than twenty miles to find a few gallons of filthy water, fit enough to bear home on their donkey's backs.

Everywhere death stalked the blasted, barren land.

And within my spirit there was the relentless pain at the plight of my people.

Wherever I went, wherever I camped in the thin shade of a thorn tree, wherever I met a Masai with his suffering animals, my soul was shot through with arrows of agony.

I had been a livestock man. I knew the disaster of drought. I had felt the anguish of losing lambs and ewes to disease or predators. I had struggled against the stern ravages and cruel reverses of nature's fickle changes.

So when my Masai despaired so did I. When they grieved in silence so did I. When they pled with God for rain so did I. We were all in this crisis together, caught up in a common heartbreak.

I was so close to the suffering of my "adopted" people in those days, so totally immersed in the dreadful drama of their despair, so completely identified with them in their peril it was as if I had in fact and in truth become a Masai myself.

I simply could not detach myself from their plight. I could not stand by as an objective observer of their terrible tragedy. I could not just, casually, make sophisticated scientific recommendations with no emotional involvement in their dilemma.

No, a thousand times no!

The same powerful, restless drive and energy which previously had been used to attain my own ends in life were now being redirected into the interests of my Masai friends. Every month I made dusty safaris into new areas. With relentless zeal I made detailed surveys of all sorts of terrain. I made copious notes and lengthy reports on soil conditions, vegetation, water supplies, livestock and game populations as well as the movements of the people themselves.

Steadily and surely critical data was gathered upon which eventually sound scientific solutions could be based for the healing of this lovely land.

What I did not then realize was that the agony of my emotions, the acute suffering of my spirit were taking a toll of my health and strength. In subtle ways the vitality and robust stamina that had been built up by our vigorous life at "Fairwinds" were being dissipated in the desperate heat of Masailand—not just climatic heat, which in some of my safari camps was almost unbearable, but the even more enervating heat of a suffering soul in the turmoil of dark times.

The paradox which compounded my personal anguish was the growing awareness that the Masai themselves seemed totally helpless to alter the direction of their own downward drift. On every side their age-old practices of primitive animal husbandry only complicated their crisis. Yet they could not seem to see the cause nor understand the consequences.

It was then that I turned to the camera to make an actual visual record of the deterioration at work in the biota. Such scenes as massive soil erosion, the desiccation of ground cover by habitual burning, the pollution of water supplies, the extinction of grass species by overgrazing, the ravages of livestock diseases on healthy herds could all be shown clearly on a screen.

To my surprise the Masai, even in the most remote manyattas, responded enthusiastically to the one-man slide shows I gave after the sun had set over the western hills. Because my vehicle was light in color the pictures were projected onto the side of the station wagon from a small compact lamp that ran off the battery.

In years to come I was to give hundreds of illustrated lectures to all sorts of sophisticated audiences. But never was any group half as enthusiastic as my Masai friends had been. They would laugh, scream in delight, and hold my hands back from advancing the slides until they identified every person, place or animal in the picture.

I realized that for a people as intelligent and alert as the Masai, the use of visual aids and firsthand demonstration of improved land management could be a formidable factor for their future benefit. This was but another means that might be used to great advantage in reversing the destructive forces at work in their society.

It should be said here that I had enormous respect for the Masai intelligence. They were a people of unusual alertness. Their youths who attended the government schools had excellent scholastic records. Some went on to take advanced higher education abroad. There were Masai with degrees from Oxford and Cambridge universities.

Unfortunately, much of the education to which they were exposed had been purely academic in content. My contention was that classes in soil conservation, land management, animal husbandry and resource use would have been a hundred times more useful to the tribe as a whole. To this end I strongly advocated the establishment of experimental areas and demonstration sites where improved scientific techniques could be carried out before their very eyes. In this visible way they would quickly realize the enormous potential for improved production that lay within their grasp.

Regular reports and in-depth studies of all sorts were submitted to the authorities. These were accepted with interest and courtesy. But little by little it also became apparent to me that many of the plans would never be put into practice simply because of the political complications then plaguing Kenya as a result of the Mau Mau emergency.

Money, men and resources which might otherwise have been available to launch some excellent schemes among the Masai were diverted instead to fighting terrorists in the forests and on the farms. The fury of the terrorist attacks was increasing. Even the aged Scottish settler twenty-seven miles from our home was butchered in his own bedroom. So the whole country was tense and taut.

In such an atmosphere the conservation cause commanded little attention.

It was a classic case, so common in the chaotic history of the human race, that guns and bullets took precedence over improved land or better lives for the common people. Because I had not yet learned to fully trust my heavenly Father with such momentous matters, the tragedy of the bloodshed lay heavy upon my spirit . . . pressing down with great weight upon my hopes for the future of the Masai.

The Mau Mau Emergency

IT IS INDEED A GREAT MERCY that God has so arranged our lives that we cannot foresee the future. Many of us would not move from the comfort or convenience of our situation to step out boldly to do His bidding if we knew what lay ahead. It is a special part of faith in Him to believe without flinching that, because He holds the future in His great strong hands, all will be well as we follow Him.

Increasingly this was the case for Phyllis and me in Masailand. For as the months moved along, twin forces of mounting pressure began to exert enormous pressure upon our private lives. In fact, they put us in very real, mortal peril.

Not that we were reluctant to lay down our lives for the Masai. We were not. This issue had been resolved and settled between us by mutual agreement long before leaving Canada. And now, having entered fully into the pitiful plight of our Masai with enormous empathy, I knew to a very acute degree exactly what Paul meant when he declared his willingness to die, if need be, that his own people might be saved.

The formidable forces which we faced were increasing illness for both of us in our isolation, and the imminence of an attack from Mau Mau terrorists.

One day I came into the house to find Phyllis had suddenly collapsed in a heap on the floor. Her symptoms baffled me, even though from early childhood I had suffered from many tropical diseases and knew their effects firsthand.

179

After months and months of drought the equatorial rains had just broken upon us. In one five-hour period alone seven inches of rain poured down out of black clouds. The storm had totally cut us off. Every donga was running full with flood water. The great plains had become a quagmire of mud that no vehicle like mine could traverse.

In stark simplicity the children and I bowed our heads and besought our Father to spare the life of our precious one. We had no telephone, no radio contact, no road to a hospital.

At dawn I sent off an African runner with a note to the Hindu doctor thirty miles away. To his unbounded credit he came, the last seven miles on foot, to declare that Phyllis had acute typhoid. It turned out his diagnosis was faulty. And it was not until several weeks later, when she could finally be moved to Nairobi, that it was found she had a most rare and virulent form of malaria. In due course she recovered, but her strength was diminished.

My own health deteriorated steadily. Many nights, because of excruciating pains in my upper torso, sleep was impossible. I would rise from bed, light a coal oil lantern, and absorb myself in writing. The flicker of its soft glow would be the only mark of human activity across miles of dark Masai terrain.

The old, unrelenting, undeviating determination to put my thoughts, experiences and hopes on paper had never diminished. Amid the anguish of my suffering this work went on steadily . . . night after night . . . often between 2:00 A.M. and the break of day.

Fortunately for both me and my family I was not fully aware how grave my illness was, nor how little time remained. Phyllis, a woman of serene faith, of enormous confidence in Christ, trusted God to direct our decisions. One of these was for me to finally go and see a devout, aged, Christian doctor who had practiced in Kenya most of his life.

His diagnosis was very simple, very straightforward: "You are one of those people who cannot live in the tropics. If you remain here, you will be buried in about six months. For the sake of your family, and for God's sake, you should return to a cool climate."

Running parallel with these decisions was the rising crescendo of the Mau Mau terrorism. When we first came to the country the killing gangs had been rampaging only in the more settled and forested areas of the highlands. But under attack from the British militia the terrorist groups began to fan out across the country in subversive activity.

The government authorities sent me confidential memos to the effect that some gangs were infiltrating Masai territory. Not only did they do this to elude the military sweeps, but also to kill game and thus provide their forces with high protein food for fighting.

As is common in the African bush, somber news began to filter through to us along the human underground communication lines. Numerous "hunting" parties of Mau Mau terrorists were in our area. They had been spotted by Masai out herding their stock.

To our amazement, the elders from the nearby villages came to see me. Out of deep respect and profound affection for us they offered to send a retinue of their warriors to sleep up at our home as a bodyguard. This action moved us deeply. Little did we realize how deep were the bonds of love and affection that had been built between us.

Equally astonishing was the quiet, sure, fearless faith shown by Phyllis in the face of such danger. For the gangs were utterly ruthless. They swept in to attack without notice. Both women and children as well as men were butchered, maimed and mutilated in cold blood and brutal bestiality.

Because their forces were so heavily committed to action elsewhere, the authorities could send us no police protection. Yet being fully aware of our great peril they insisted on sending me two tough game scouts fully armed.

I had all the wild brush and scrub thorn within a 300-yard radius of the house cut down and cleared away. This would forestall a sneak attack. I procured two fine big Alsatians as guard dogs—Duke and Dell. The Masai marveled at their size and strength, calling them, "The young lions."

I slept with a flashlight and fully loaded .303 rifle at my bedside. Phyllis slept with a Masai machete at her side. And because the Masai had long since learned I could drop a Thompson's gazelle with a single shot at more than 300 yards, the word had gone out, *"Don't fool with this fellow!"*

From boyhood I had learned, the hard way, that the best

defense is a good offense. So with my two armed scouts, from time to time, I would make a sweeping foray across the country in the dark of night to raid the Mau Mau hunting camps. We would rush them in the night, firing shots into the ground around them, taking them totally by surprise before they could react.

In this way scores of them were taken into custody. All their weapons were confiscated. The game meat they had butchered was seized, and the plains in our area had peace.

In typical African fashion I was soon honored with the name *"Bwana Kifagiro"*—"Mr. Broom"—because I had swept our district clear of the gangs. This was no light thing to do. All the hunters were armed with bows and arrows tipped with lethal poison. A single shaft sunk in my body would have done its deadly work. Some of those arrows are still in their handmade leather quiver, standing in my study today.

Amid all this armed activity, we still recognized that our final safety depended upon the care and protection of our Father. And, as Phyllis used to remark to me so often: "God's child is immortal as long as God has work for him to do in this wicked, old world."

So, without fanfare or flamboyancy we lived quietly as a family, making the most of each day granted to us by God.

The Mau Mau uprising eventually was suppressed by the British authorities. Jomo Kenyatta, who had spent most of the time in prison, was released to become Kenya's first president in an independent territory. With acute foresight he was intelligent enough to recognize that the country could only be restored to prosperity with the help of white people.

Because of his remarkable turnabout in policy that actually encouraged Europeans to remain and work in a multiracial society, Kenya stands today as one of the most viable of all African states. But the price paid was appalling in bloodshed and bitter losses.

The African church went through horrendous suffering. Christians were murdered, burned to death in their huts and driven to flee for their lives. It was a period of enormous pain and persecution for God's people. Yet its end-result was to purify and cleanse the entire body of believers—so much so that those who survived the terrible times emerged to establish one of the most virile communities of Christians to be found anywhere in the world.

At the time of "the terror" it seemed most unlikely that Kenya would survive its blood bath. But it did. No small measure of the credit for this is due to the impassioned, persistent prayers of the Africans themselves. In an acute awareness that it would require a miracle of divine intervention, Christians sought God's strength and wisdom for solutions to their impasse. In my own numerous contacts with enlightened Africans I was encouraged to see their humble dependence on God for guidance. With such an attitude I was sure the future could be brighter than the awful darkness we then endured.

The only thing that troubled me profoundly was an awareness that time was running out to reverse some of the trends set in motion by the Mau Mau emergency. For one thing Kenya was shorn of any funds for assisting the Masai.

For that reason I turned to the authorities in Tanganyika (Tanzania) to see if perchance a pilot scheme, such as had been envisioned for Kenya, might be established there among the Masai. It was a last, faltering attempt to do something tangible before my fragile health collapsed completely.

At their invitation I went down to make an initial survey of a possible site very close to the Kenya border. Because of interterritorial regulations I was not permitted to take any weapons with me on this excursion.

After meeting with the officials and going over their maps carefully I decided to go out into the terrain in mind and make camp there. I could then cover it on foot in a detailed survey.

With my binoculars I found a spring. It stood out because of the dense vegetation growing at the head of a donga. So I drove across country with infinite care and parked carefully in the shade of an acacia. It was just getting dusk. As I walked toward the spring several natives scurried off through the thick bush.

In the usual, amiable manner of strangers I called out a greeting. There was no reply. Only the distant sound of their movement in the undergrowth. It seemed very strange.

Drawing a pot of water from the spring I strolled back

to the car. There I gathered some dry wood, built a small camp fire, and prepared my simple supper of roast lamb ribs. Grilled over the glowing coals, they were delicious.

Sitting alone by the fire, the African night all around me, I knew I was at a crucial crossroad in life. Would God open another door in Tanganyika for us as He had in Kenya? Or was my work, my time, my tears, my agony for the Masai almost at an end? What would tomorrow bring?

With thoughts such as these moving across my mind I decided to simply stretch out in the back of the station wagon and sleep. It had been a long day. Slumber came swiftly.

Suddenly about 2:00 A.M. I was startled wide awake with a bright light shining full in my face. Someone was hammering on the window above my head.

My immediate, subconscious response, from months of intense mental preparedness was—"It's a Mau Mau attack!" But I was utterly helpless, unarmed, alone—trapped in my vehicle. This was the end!

I sat bolt upright, feeling for my .303 rifle that was not there, groping for my hunting knife that I had never even thought to lay beside me in this "safe" territory.

Out of the blinding light a deep guttural voice challenged me in English. "Why aren't you dead? Why aren't you dead?" It didn't make sense.

I was being scrutinized in total disbelief by a tough South African police officer. In staccato, rapid-fire sentences he quickly told me that just that day his unit had been sent into this remote terrain to make a sweep for Mau Mau terrorists. It was the first gang to cross into Tanganyika from Kenya, and they had encamped by this very spring.

"Did you know you were surrounded by about forty-two terrorists in the night?" he asked me, raising his eyebrows. "We have either killed or captured twenty-six since our attack at midnight!" He held his breath as if in utter amazement. "I just don't believe they would leave you here alone, alive!"

I ran my fingers through my tousled hair. Rubbing the sleep from my eyes I simply looked at him calmly and replied: "Sir, I am a child of God. My heavenly Father has set His guardian angel to keep watch over me here this night."

The burly officer grunted in disbelief. "Well, you can't

stay here. At dawn emergency regulations will apply here, as they do in Kenya."

The next day I conferred again with the now highly agitated local authorities.

"We are sorry, Mr. Keller, but under these critical circumstances any plans we, or you, have for the Masai must be postponed indefinitely."

Clearly, dramatically the door had been closed!

Wildlife Studies

When I returned from Tanganyika, Phyllis and I realized that some very hard decisions had to be made. It was obvious that because of circumstances beyond our control, much that we had hoped to achieve in the country would have to be deferred. At least *Stage* 1 and *Stage* 2 of our basic strategy had been carried through to completion.

We had become very attached to our Masai people. They in turn had demonstrated by their actions a remarkable acceptance of us as their friends. Consistently, gently, quietly we shared the Good News of our Father's love in Christ with them. There had been the usual, cordial nonresistance. They were noncommittal in their response. Yet we were confident the day would come when God would honor His own Word shared with many of them. Subsequent events have shown this to be so.

Similarly we had to exercise sufficient faith in the special sovereignty of our God to believe quietly that in His own good time, in His own gracious way, the work for which we had laid the foundation in all our surveys would be built upon by others. I was thoroughly familiar with missionary enterprise all over the earth through study and reading. Again and again good men and brave women had laid down their lives without seeing any spectacular results. Yet subsequently others would follow in their footsteps to harvest bountiful returns for the Master.

Finally there remained the formidable fact that because of our fragile health, it was essential to return to a cooler climate. The dear, godly, insightful physician had put it to me very forcibly. "Phillip, under God, your first responsibility is to provide properly for your wife and children—not the Masai." He looked me straight in the eyes. "Keep your priorities in proper order, young man!"

So often Christian workers have literally consumed themselves in service to their people, causing their own wives and children to be the losers. I had tasted a little of this treatment as a small child and knew well its bitter effects.

Because of all these combined events which steadily closed in around us, it was decided our full term of service, now concluded with the authorities, should be our last. It was a tough choice. Arrangements were made at once to fly Phyllis and the children back to Canada. Lynn had reached school age. She would need to be enrolled in classes. Out in the bush, both Phyllis and I had already given her extensive basic instructions in many courses.

For my part, there remained a burning desire to make a final photographic record of the major wildlife species of the area. Meticulous notes, numerous field observations and in-depth studies of animal behavior had already been made. In fact, they were among the first serious wildlife studies ever done in this district. And when my work was brought to the attention of Dr. George Petrides from Michigan State University he came to see me at once. He had been commissioned to make basic recommendations for wildlife management in Kenya.

He and I became friends. In due course we made an expedition together to climb Mt. Kilimanjaro. Camped in a cave one night at about 14,000 feet elevation, he there challenged me mightily. "Phillip, the great gap in human communication is between technical theoretical knowledge and language laymen can understand." The glow from the flames of our camp fire flickered across his face. "If you can take sophisticated data and put it into language the lay person on the street understands, it is the most noble service you can perform." He weighed his words carefully. "Few can do this in any field!"

God used his remarks in that cold, chill, dark cave high

on Kilimanjaro to challenge my will and redirect my work for the rest of my days. It was a new spur to drive me on, more determined than ever, to put on paper, in language laymen could grasp, the titanic truths of scientific discovery.

Little did I then realize how eventually God would use the same identical principle, in my Christian writing, to present truths of spiritual revelation in a simple way for lay people to grasp.

The day we came down off that mountain, back to the hot Masai plains at its base, I knew surely the future area of endeavor in which my life work would lie—provided, of course, that I even survived my increasing illness.

The day came for Phyllis and the children to leave. In a deeply moving, touching, tender gesture of farewell the Masai came up in a steady stream to bid them farewell. There were tears. There were last touches of love. There was even a magnificent big lamb presented as a parting gift. "You are going on a long, long journey," they insisted, pressing their gift upon her. "And you and the children will need food, flesh, meat, for strength along the way. Here it is!"

When finally the plane lifted off at dawn, a deep tug pulled at my heart. The separation was not easy. I would be on my own in my safari camps for several more months. I was staying the maximum time the doctor said my health could stand the strain. Urgent work remained to be done. My family were now safe elsewhere. Without reserve I could fling myself wholeheartedly into the final wildlife studies.

In a stirring vindication of the work we had done among the Masai, two leaders of the mission who would not have us initially, came to see me. They had heard of our efforts. Now as field representatives they invited us to join them. It was too late! The die had been cast. Yet it remained a quiet consolation to know our work for Christ had not been in vain . . . nor gone unnoticed.

Our home on the plains was emptied. Loading what simple, basic safari gear I needed into my vehicle, I drove off into the "blue." My shelter now would be only a bush tent. Every meal for months would be cooked over an open campfire. A canvas safari cot would be the only bed for my weakened body. From dawn to dark I would move and live quietly among the Masai, among the flat-topped acacia trees, among the wildlife that made up such a magnificent part of the African scene.

This book makes no attempt to describe in detail the exciting episodes or amazing adventures experienced during those days. That has all been done with love and empathy in my previous books, *Africa's Wild Glory* and *Splendour from the Land,* published in such superb format by Jarrolds of London, England.

Yet it is incumbent upon me to tell something of those remarkable interludes simply to preserve the pathos of this period in my life. Also it is essential to share a little of the profound spiritual struggles which were mine in the solitude of so many of my safari camps. All alone under the stars of the African night, there were long, quiet hours during which God, by His Spirit, had a unique opportunity to commune with me in the depths of my spirit.

I have never been a man to shun solitude. Quite the opposite. I relish those still interludes, those gentle hours, when alone with Christ, He is given time and opportunity to speak to me privately, personally. And I have always sensed His special intimacy in those hours when I was farthest removed from the pressing clamor of the busy, boisterous society of man. Most often this has been in some remote camp, beyond the hills, beside some stream or mountain spring, perhaps at the ocean edge.

I can readily identify with men like Moses, Elijah, John the Baptist or John the Beloved, to whom God revealed Himself in special measure during their "desert days." The silence of my safari days was a precious, poignant chance for God to speak to me.

My major difficulty has ever been that a serious, sober sense of responsibility in service always intrudes itself between myself and my Master. Part of this, of course, is because of the intense discipline and strict upbringing of my parents who placed enormous emphasis upon "perfect performance." Part is because of the rigid regimentation instilled by the schools I attended. Part is sheer personal pride in achievement . . . the "success syndrome."

Combined, they constitute a formidable force in life that drives an individual to devote himself wholeheartedly to any endeavor. So I was to fling myself fully and unflinchingly into wildlife studies, just as previously I had done it with land use, ranch management and Masai matters.

In a word—the service always came before the Savior.

My priorities were backwards. It would take years to get them into proper perspective.

At this point in my career there had already been conferred upon me a great honor by the Kenya government. Because of my intense interest in wildlife preservation I had been appointed an Honorary Game Warden. My natural love for animals and increasing knowledge of their behavior began to attract considerable attention. It surprised the wildlife people from abroad who began to take an interest in my work with wild species.

Part of this was because of the photographic record being compiled with painstaking persistence. When we first returned to Kenya I had almost always gone into the field armed with a high-powered rifle, and accompanied by at least one native tracker. This was the traditional way of stalking or hunting so-called "dangerous" big game, such as lion, buffalo, rhino, leopard or elephant.

Though I carried a camera and was primarily intent on taking pictures, I always assured myself that if an extreme emergency arose and I was suddenly attacked, I could always "shoot my way out" of the sticky situation.

Quickly I discovered that this was a false premise on which to work with wildlife. There were two main reasons. The first was the fact that both my tracker and myself were inclined to be tense. Often the anxiety expressed itself in either overly aggressive or apprehensive behavior on our part. This was immediately transmitted to the animals which reacted in fear and often fled.

I remember so clearly the first close encounter with a herd of elephants in very dense brush. My tracker was so alarmed by their sudden appearance that when I glanced around to see his reaction, I found he was already fifteen feet up a nearby tree.

The second cause for disappointing results with wildlife lay in the rifle. I began to leave it in camp, along with my native tracker, and go out alone unarmed, at ease, relaxed with an attitude of patience and empathy for the animals. I simply could not rush things.

The results were astonishing and dramatic. I saw now that there was an increasing rapport between the animals and myself. There was no sense of threat between us. I came among them as a quiet, compassionate observer of their habits. They were my friends, not my quarry.

An even more remarkable discovery was to find that once I was within voice range, I could talk to them in an intimate, cordial way. Their response was amazing, reassuring. Partly, this might have been because of my low-pitched, evenly modulated voice. Partly, it was because through my voice I could convey to them my interest and empathy for them. Partly, just as with an owner and his pet, my voice was used to transmit my enormous pleasure and contentment at being in their company. They relished this and relaxed in my presence.

Fortunately for me, the particular model of Leica camera I purchased had an unusually smooth, quiet shutter mechanism. So when I took pictures the very slight camera noise scarcely disturbed the animals. Combined with this it was a compact, light piece of equipment, which, even when mounted with a 135 mm. lens, could be carried easily anywhere I went—even climbing trees to get better views.

Steadily my studies, especially of the big-game species, took on an aura of adventure, discovery and pleasure beyond my fondest hopes. Actually I was breaking new ground in my field. For, single-handedly without the benefit of elaborate safari expeditions, or the outlay of enormous sums of money, I was obtaining insights into animal behavior never recorded before.

This was doubly astonishing because of the territory and terrain in which I worked. I was not in national parks where animals become familiar with people and thus lose some of their fear for man. Nor was I in any sort of sanctuary set apart for the safety and preservation of wildlife. Rather I was studying herds of elephants, prides of lions, rhino, buffalo and even leopards where they were hunted by white hunters, harassed by African poachers, or sometimes pursued by Masai spearmen set on settling an old score.

The whole enterprise became enthralling. I knew the thrills of intimate interludes in which an entire day would be spent approaching closer and closer to my prey. By sundown I would be shooting a magnificent-maned lion from about eight feet away. This made my blood race with sheer delight. Other times I have sat up in small trees observing elephants, waiting until they actually fed off the foliage of the branches around me. So close were they to my boots that I was only twelve or fourteen feet from the tip of their sensitive trunks.

I have spent hours working my way closer and closer to a rhino until I could toss a twig on the tip of his nostrils ten feet away, as he stretched out leisurely in a favorite dust-bath. In all of this I was rapidly learning that the magnificent specimens I lived and worked with were compassionate, adaptable creatures who asked only to live in serenity.

It should be remembered that all of this was long before people like Joy Adamson and her pet lioness, Elsa, gave the civilized world an intimate insight into wild animal behavior. *Born Free* alerted a whole generation to the plight of Africa's animals.

For me as a man, there was a bittersweet dimension to all that I was doing. It needs to be mentioned here. Yet I do not intend to belabor the point unduly.

The bitter part was an increasing awareness that wildlife would not, could not, long survive in Africa under ever-mounting human demands for land, water and vegetation. The only place the great concentrations of wild animals could hope to endure would be within the sanctuary of national parks. Even there, their plight could be precarious under the political upheavals which are so great a part of the unstable African scene. Recent events in Uganda and Ethiopia, for example, show how vulnerable parks are when ravaged by ruthless gangs bent on slaughter.

All of this I sensed and knew more than thirty years ago. Because of it I pled with both the authorities and the Masai to recognize the remarkable resource they owned in their native wildlife. I urged them to cherish, preserve and protect it as their finest investment for the future.

The sweet side to my wildlife interludes were the exquisite pleasure and personal rewards of inner satisfaction they gave me. All my boyhood dreams of being a game warden, a field naturalist, a wildlife photographer had been completely fulfilled. The results were dramatic. The books and photographs illustrating them that would emerge from these early beginnings in the "blue" would command international attention. The wind of God's Spirit had been at work in all of this!

One day Dr. George Petrides would write to me personally and say: "Phillip, the ground work of conservation you laid in Kenya is coming to life at last, especially in Masailand. You were the first to envision it!"

This was, in its own way, part of God's gentle compensation to me for the anguish and agony endured. It would help ease the pain in parting again from a land I loved with such intensity.

The Close of a Chapter

As WEEK FOLLOWED WEEK in my safari camps, an acute aware-ness came over me that I stood now at the end of a bittersweet chapter in my life. The tale of the years spent among the Masai had been written in tears and in pain, but also in re-markable events of joyous adventure never to be forgotten.

During that interlude mother had gone home to be with her Lord, whom she loved so profoundly. In the back flyleaf of her well-worn Bible were written these few lines:

> "It is God who brought me here.
> It is God who has kept me here.
> It is God who will lead me on from here."

They exactly expressed my own innermost convictions. The future now was unsure. Yet in the anguish of again leav-ing the land I loved so much I was sure He would show the way I should take. In that quiet confidence lay peace and repose.

In Canada I had lost my land.

In Kenya I had lost my health.

But always there remained the acute awareness that God, by the presence of His gracious Spirit, was actually at work in my affairs. I had not lost Him.

Surely, steadily, a massive manuscript had been written describing many of the exciting episodes among the Masai.

Perhaps it would provide the proper material for a "first book." I had been in touch with a leading New York publishing house about it. They seemed keen to see both the written material and accompanying photographs.

It was a mere "straw in the wind" during those final days in the bush. But eventually it was to prove, when caught up in the wonder of the wind of God's Spirit, to become a pivotal point in my life. For little is much when God is in it.

My last night in Africa had arrived. The years in Masailand were at an end. At dawn of the next day my plane would lift off the Nairobi runway to hoist me high across the continent, back to Canada—back to a land of cold, clean air where perhaps my broken body could mend itself once more.

For the past five months I had lived alone among the Masai. I had slept on a cot under canvas or else merely rolled up in my sleeping bag under the stars. This I had chosen to do purposely that I might enter more deeply and intimately into the secret heart of a land I loved so intensely.

Those were precious months. Each day I hugged to myself knowing full well that perhaps never again would I enjoy the liberty of living so freely with a people I adored, while still they were unspoiled by civilization. Nor again would there be a chance to turn back the clock and revel in an Africa which was altering at an astonishing pace—an Africa of open plains, unfenced horizons, wild game and carefree days under the sun.

The previous night I had spent out in the bush in my camp perched on the banks of a broad sand river. There the river bed lay a shimmering strand under its own magic moon. Upon that silver stage I had watched ten tuskers come down to drink. Shoulder to shoulder they stood in rank as though presenting a final salute. It moved me mightily. When their dark bulks had disappeared into the shadows a little of my soul went with them.

From the soil at my feet I had picked up a handful of Africa's earth. It was earth that was rich and fertile. It had produced a wild glory all its own, but it had been trampled, abused and bled by careless men until now it cried for relief.

Slowly I had let the sandy soil trickle through my fingers. An eddy of night air carried it away in a tiny cloud of dust.

Yes, time too was running out for this land, just as this earth ran through my open fingers. There would not be much more opportunity to heal this land and restore its spirit if present trends continued.

Heavy at heart, I had turned from the river and walked back to sit by my campfire—unable to sleep. This was not surprising. This was the final, long look at the "bush" under moonlight. It was the culmination of a short career that I had hoped would last so much longer. It was the fork in the trail. Tomorrow I would go back to Nairobi—back to the civilization I disliked so intensely, and back to the roar of traffic and the madness of modern man.

And now there I was, back in that whirlpool. My last night in Africa, how would it be spent? Just at sundown the telephone rang. It was one of my African friends, phoning to see if he could come up for a final visit and chat. Of course I was delighted; why shouldn't I be? I held Musa in the highest esteem. He wondered if he might bring some friends. Naturally, it would be splendid to meet them.

Musa was, like myself, a comparatively young man, who had come up through my father's schools, then gravitated to Nairobi in search of further opportunities for his alert mind. In fact, he was actually the pastor of the small church in Nairobi erected by the Africans as a memorial to my father. It was there we first met, and from that first meeting Musa and I took to each other instinctively.

Subsequent years saw greater and greater responsibilities placed upon Musa. He was destined to become the first African cabinet minister ever to sit in the Kenya legislative council. Eventually it was he who was chosen to voice and declare the position of East Africa to a bewildered, Western world in a series of lectures which he conducted at some of our leading universities.

But this last night of which I write, Musa came with his companions almost as if in secret. His fellows were city aldermen, editorial staff and other leaders of the African community. They came from Uganda and various parts of Kenya. Musa was a Marigoli, two of his companions were Kikuyu, another a Buganda, another a Luo and one a Nandi.

They arrived about eight o'clock and immediately we launched into a spirited discussion of African affairs. After all, it was rare indeed in those days for an African to sit thus in a European home and discuss on a par the problems of his own people.

Our topics ranged from politics to the price of posho; from life insurance to life expectancy under modern medicine; from religion to rhinos; from Livingstone to Leakey.

Before we realized it the hands of the clock showed 2 A.M. My plane was due to leave within three hours. The night had simply melted away under the heat of our enthusiasm and happy comradeship. Earnestly and sincerely I urged them to have courage for their cause, for Africa's destiny lay surely in their own hands.

They rose to leave and one of them turned to me with the remark: "Mr. Keller, you are more African than an African!"

It was one of the finest compliments I had ever been paid. In that precious moment of time I felt fully rewarded for all the anguish of spirit that had been mine during the past two years. Nothing, absolutely nothing now could ever make me believe that it had been in vain.

The dusky men walked out into the blackness of the African night; possibly none of us would ever meet again; we were . . . "ships that passed in the night."

The little charter plane in which I had chosen to fly to London lifted off the runway just as gray dawn streaked the eastern sky. As we climbed and circled over the patchwork of Kikuyu farms, wattle groves and coffee plantations, I could see Mount Kenya silhouetted against the sun's red flare.

We slipped across the high Kikuyu escarpment, and in the pale morning light I felt sure I could just barely discern the great, gray building of the school on the hill where most of my early book learning had been done. It lay in the misty embrace of the brooding forest where as a boy I would stalk the plantain-eaters and Colobus monkeys of the hills.

Now we were out over the yawning trench of the Rift Valley. European ranches, fence lines and wheat fields formed a pattern on the valley floor where formerly I had known only herds of zebra, wildebeest and kongoni . . . with dust devils spiraling across the flats in crazy contortions.

On and on we droned, passing between the extinct, old craters of Suswa to the south and Longonot to the north.

This was Masailand again and looking down ahead of the wing's leading edge I could see the circles of thorn corrals lying warm and cozy in the golden sun that splashed over the barren hills.

Tiny plumes of dust puffed up around black lines of dots that trickled out of the corrals. The herds were being taken out to pasture again on the brown, eroded hills. Everywhere deep gashes showed where trails had washed into gullies, and the earth, under the incredible cutting of numberless hooves, was raw and red.

From the hills we passed on over the somber scene of a gray sea—gray with the terrible tide of leleleshwe that spread farther across the land each year. Where fifty years ago this was a country clothed richly in grass, now only the gray peril persisted.

On and on north and west we flew; below us the Loita plains, now parched and white, faded into the thick bush of the Trans Mara region. Here that pesky little creature, so detested by man, the tsetse fly, held sway. Here the bush was verdant, the grass thick, the streams ran clear and game abounded. I saw a small herd of elephants moving between the trees. A few giraffes stood in a clearing. A lovely stream meandered through the savanna down toward the lake which lay ahead.

That was my last—my very last glimpse of Masailand. In a few minutes we were out over the edge of Lake Victoria, soon to send our shadow skimming across its blue and tranquil surface.

A few days later, such is the speed of modern travel, I was in the heart of New York discussing the manuscript and photographs with the editorial board of the publisher I had corresponded with in Kenya. They could see I was a very ill man. I had dragged myself back from the very brink; so they urged me to return quietly to be reunited with my family.

In due course I would hear from them.

It so happened Christmas was approaching. So I pushed on for the west coast. The festive season would be celebrated around the family hearth amid the chill winter of Canada's biting cold.

The joy of being with Phyllis and the children again after so long a separation was the only consolation for my bodily weakness. I had come back a wreck of a man. Many mornings I was too ill, too weak, too immobilized even to rise from bed.

As is usual in such cases, all sorts of kindly, well-meaning advice came to us from friends, neighbors and family. I was urged to seek medical help. A number of doctors were recommended. Various kinds of diets were suggested.

Somehow there was no inclination on my part to be caught up in any complex medical rehabilitation. A deep inner instinct reassured me that given time, ample fresh air, simple food, sunshine, tranquillity and moderate exercise my body could mend itself.

Here was a chance to test that belief. I decided not to see a doctor at all and gave myself six full months in which to concentrate on nothing else but getting well.

Besides the garden I found another form of invigoration in the city swimming pool. It being winter, sea bathing was not attractive, though even in midsummer most of the waters around Victoria are too cold to encourage prolonged swimming. Each afternoon I would take a moderate swim, comfortably entwined with drowsy sessions standing under the warm, relaxing showers. The lifeguard at the pool became a close friend whose practical advice on exercise and simple diet stood me in good stead. He was a tough, colorful character whose fine physique betrayed his own hard life, part of which had been spent in the dust and heat of Mesopotamia.

Slowly but inexorably I sensed strength seeping back into my body. As winter passed on into spring I found that I could work longer in the garden. In fact, I gradually grew quite energetic and started to tear out old ramblers, cut down trees, trim hedges and have hopping, big fires to burn up the brush I thus accumulated.

At the pool I began to take longer and longer swims, doing more and more lengths each week. I also found a fresh zest in practicing and perfecting some of the intricate high dives that had always fascinated me before.

Spring, which comes ever so gently and almost unnoticed on the island, soon made an impact on the garden and on my spirits. It was a treat to welcome the sun back in strength again. I would walk along the shore, gathering bark for the fireplace, watching the gulls wheel, cry, quarrel and scavenge the tideline for food. I would seek a sheltered nook in the sun behind some log or rock and there doze in the warmth to dream dreams of the Africa I had left behind.

I could only dream back in memory during those days. For the future was a nebulous, hazy unknown in which were mingled hope and despair: hope because some mornings I felt strong enough to believe that I would again be able to carve out a new career for myself; despair because other days I was weak and wretched with pain that made nothing but a hollow mockery of any plans I laid.

But gradually—ever so gradually—the good days began to outnumber the bad days. With this shift in the balance my optimism grew and my physical strength was stimulated by a brighter mental outlook.

During this time two events took place that were to have an enormous impact on the next decade of my life. First a parcel came from the New York publisher, returning all of my manuscript material, plus the photographs. With it was a terse note of rejection, added to which was this cutting comment:

"Mr. Keller, if you had spent as much time learning to be a writer, as you have enjoying these adventures, you would be quite a journalist."

The letter stabbed Phyllis with utter dismay. "Darling," she remarked, her eyes brimming with tears, "you have worked so hard at writing for all these years. It's time to give it up!"

For me the reaction was just the opposite. Like a sharp spur driven into a horse's flank, it was the prod that drove me to prove my own prowess, no matter what any publisher said. I would rewrite and rearrange the material and try again.

The second significant event was the decision to send a collection of my African slides to the *National Geographic* Magazine. To my unbounded delight they met with a positive response. And a few weeks later a handsome check for $2500.00 was fluttering in my hands.

Then and there I decided that this was a new dimension of life which deserved to be developed. If necessary I would take a course in photography that would enable my writing to be illustrated with professional skill and expertise. I would even embark on producing wildlife films.

The glitter of this new and exciting field began to mesmerize me. I confess to my own chagrin and honest humiliation now, that my Father's interests and concern in the matter were not always sought as they should have been. I was drifting into a direction of my own choosing. It was dangerous!

Jaguars in the Jungle

MY CONVALESCENCE TOOK almost twice as long as I had originally planned. Instead of six months, it required about a year to recover the robust strength and bodily vigor enjoyed formerly at "Fairwinds." Still it was tremendously stimulating to me as a man to sense and feel the flow of new health that steadily replaced the debilitating diseases that had wellnigh destroyed me.

This was doubly gratifying simply because I did not resort to doctors, drugs, surgery, modern medicine or even hospital care to cure the condition. In simplicity of life style, and complete confidence in Christ's ability to place His healing touch upon my life, wholeness was restored. All of this was done without fanfare, special services, or attending any particular healing meetings.

In fairness, charity and openness I sincerely respect those who seek medical aid just as I respect those who believe in divine remedies. I am acutely aware God uses doctors, nurses and surgical science to assist those who are ill. Likewise there are cases where by implicit faith in God others have been cured.

Each person must choose the path he follows. In my case I delight to think my Father has designed my body with such incredible ingenuity that given proper care, it can not only resist disease but also repair the damage done to it. On God's part He has provided the marvelous mechanisms for health and healing to occur. For my part there remains the responsibility to eat nutritious food, drink pure drinks, expose myself to ample fresh air and sunshine, obtain adequate exercise and enjoy proper rest in order to be well.

Combined with these there must be a cheerful attitude of gratitude for all God's great benefits. There must be worthwhile work to occupy one's mind. There must be someone to love and cherish. There must be high hope for the future. There must be fun!

During the quiet months of my steady recovery I began to search for a school that could provide me with advanced photographic instruction. The main desire from my standpoint was to become well informed in the artistic aspects of this field. I was more concerned with being able to produce photographs of fine esthetic quality rather than merely manipulate highly sophisticated camera equipment.

Secondly I wanted basic, sound instruction in the production of high caliber motion pictures. For in my mind's eye there began to dawn the vision of eventually producing both beautiful books, illustrated with my own photographs, and also films of great intrinsic merit.

I have always been repelled by books, films, magazines or other forms of media that flaunted the sordid, skeptical, specious aspects of human behavior. I have real contempt for members of the publishing industry and film producers who use their media merely to make huge profits while pandering to the lowest, basest emotions in men and women.

So one of my consuming passions was to produce truly fine films and beautiful books which would stand on their own intrinsic merit, which carried such excellent content that they commanded wide recognition for their own inherent worth, which without propaganda, promotion or false flimflam would offer the public a superior choice based on a sound, wholesome Christian perspective.

With all of this in mind I finally decided to enroll in The Brooks Institute of Photography in Santa Barbara, California. They offered a short course for people like myself who were not prepared to spend years in study . . . but who wanted basic instruction in the discipline within a short time span.

A year after our return from Africa my family and I were happily settled in a little suite close to the ocean. For us it was "love at first sight" when we came to this gentle, little coastal community where "the mountains meet the sea." The lovely beaches, the magnificent gardens, the noble Santa Ynez mountains, the abundant bird life, the gentle moderate climate provided a perfect setting in which to study photography.

At the Institute I proved to be a rather unusual student. For one thing, I was much older than most of my classmates. Second, I had already done a great deal of field work with excellent results, largely because of a natural instinct for photography. Third, I was the only one who had ever come with the avowed intention to do only wildlife work. In great good humor, my associates who were into commercial work, industry, glamor or advertising kidded me a great deal.

I had been on course only a few weeks when one day the senior instructor strode into the lecture room and addressed me directly: "Keller, how would you like to go to Mexico on a major expedition to photograph jaguars in the jungle?"

Of course I was interested!

Arrangements were made to meet the sponsor of the expedition. He was a brilliant individual who had been active in the United States Navy photographic division. In fact he had designed a superb, all metal, combat movie-camera for use in action. It was terribly tough and could withstand enormous abuse.

Fortunately I carried with me a collection of my African still work when we first met. Because I had no field experience with a motion picture camera, except the first basic classes at the Institute, he seemed hesitant to take me along. But when he and his wife saw my African work they were deeply impressed.

Still he hesitated.

"I'll make you an offer," I said, trying to help him decide. "I'll do all your still work gratis. If you take me on, I simply ask for a chance to do some movie work in case there is more than your professionals from Hollywood can manage in the field."

He jumped to his feet, stretched his hand out to grip mine in a confirming handshake, and grinned widely. "You're on!"

Within forty-eight hours I had a visa for Mexico, and we were on our way south toward the coastal jungles of Mazatlan.

It soon became apparent that I was with people to whom money was merely a means to an end. Anything they desired they could procure, for they were exceedingly well-to-do.

An imposing tent camp had been set up on the banks of a large stream that flowed leisurely into a labyrinth of bayous grown thick with mangroves and native jungle. Here there was ensconced a craggy cougar-hunter from Arizona with his notorious collection of cougar hounds. Also there was a dignified old Mexican "Don," who was skilled in calling up jaguars on his well worn, hand-carved hunting horn.

Initial sorties into the mangrove swamps had shown that jaguars were plentiful. So we started at once in search of specimens to photograph in their native habitat.

The high humidity and dense undergrowth made following the hounds exhausting. Some spots we had to wade through mud and muck up to our waists. In other places a trail had to be slashed through the jungle using sharp Mexican machetes.

Increasingly the mosquitoes, flies, mud, heat and jungle conditions began to take their toll. I was glad to be as strong as I was. But my associates started to lose heart. Several of them intimated they had had enough and would prefer to go home, back to the comforts of California.

One evening, after our simple supper of Mexican camp fare, the head of the expedition called me aside privately. "I'm in need of your help, Phillip," he remarked quietly, the strain of anxiety playing upon his features. "Some of the crew are packing it in to leave." Deep furrows lined his taut face. "That leaves the filming up to you!"

Commingled emotions swept through me. On one hand it was an enormous responsibility for one not yet adequately experienced in the profession. On the other side I saw it as the opportunity of a lifetime to gain field experience in the immediate moment.

He picked up one of his finest combat cameras and thrust it into my hot hands. "Here, take it, and all I am telling you is—'Shoot—Shoot—Shoot.'" A grim resolve rumbled in his voice. "Whatever you see of interest—shoot it—jaguars, anacondas, birdlife, reptiles, scenery, insects, native activities."

It was an open mandate! There were no restrictions! It was the chance to put on film, in full color, for the first time, the fascinating primeval life of this watery jungle world. In the ensuing six weeks I put well over 13,000 feet of film through that camera. What a thrill! What a "windfall."

Yes, in truth, and in actual adventure, the wondrous wind of the Spirit of God, active in this remote jungle camp, was opening rare opportunities for me of immeasurable worth. I was keenly aware that this was no mere coincidence contrived by the random events of time. It was, instead, a precise path prepared for me by my Father in His own wondrous way.

There were deeply moving interludes in that jungle setting. Even as I recall them now, more than a quarter century later, the recollection sends shivers up my spine. There was the warm, steamy morning, when a female jaguar, glowing gold and black in her shining spotted coat, moved so stealthily through the dappled jungle light. Scattered sunlight, falling through the overhead canopy of mangrove leaves and branches, provided the pristine backdrops against which the magnificent creature moved in lithe beauty and strength. Because of her spangled rosettes she blended in utter loveliness with her background . . . a picture of divine design.

There was the night of the full moon when the old "Don" and I drifted silently along the bayou in our crude native dugout canoe. The plaintive mating call of his hunting horn carried far across the velvet stillness of the silvered night. Suddenly there was a heavy splash. A magnificent male jaguar began to swim strongly toward us. His majestic head, breaking the quiet surface of the water, left behind a stream of bubbles on the mirror surface of the lagoon.

Suddenly at less than thirty feet from our gunwhale he saw he had been seduced by our false mating call. With enormous dignity he turned, swam to a nearby rise of ground and rose to stand in regal splendor bathed in silver light. Even the old "Don" shook his hoary head in awe and amazement. In all his years he had never seen such wild glory.

So day followed night, and night followed day in the ongoing excitement of our expedition. I had almost forgotten I was supposed to be on a course of instruction at The Brooks

Institute. Then at last, my field work done, the proper time had come to return to Santa Barbara. I flew back to try to pick up on the lectures missed.

A few weeks later the expedition leader called me to meet him at the film studios in Hollywood. The footage had turned out better than our highest hopes or loftiest dreams. It was utterly superb. He was ecstatic with delight and appreciation!

"Keller, you have done a magnificent job!" His eyes shone and sparkled with satisfaction. "As a mark of my genuine gratitude I am giving you, as a gift, the combat camera and all the equipment you used in Mexico." My heart skipped a beat or two. It seemed almost too good to be true. "What is more, I want to offer you a top salary to be my cameraman in photographing big game around the world—Kodiak bears in Alaska, the snow leopard in Asia. . . ."

This was heady stuff for one so new to movie-making. But my more immediate question was, "What about my course at the Institute?" I went to see Mr. Brooks, Sr. who had founded the school of photography. He was a big-hearted, genial, ardent outdoorsman. After hearing my account of the expedition he stood to his feet, came around his desk, put his strong arm around my shoulder and remarked with a wide smile:

"Phillip, you learned more in the jungles of Mexico than we could ever teach you here. We will grant you your diploma just as if you had taken the full course!"

It was an enthusiastic, aroused, recharged man who a few months later returned to Canada, dreaming great dreams of wildlife photography. Again, as in my second year of university life, I had experienced the enormous stimulation of energetic enthusiasm which is such a hallmark of the American way of life. The sky was the limit. It was a society of unbounded vision.

Behind me, almost forgotten in my fresh aspirations, were the agony of losing "Fairwinds," the anguish of leaving Masailand, the recent attrition of broken hopes and broken health.

It seemed as though I had rebounded to my feet once more, though knocked flat to the floor again and again.

Dad had often said to me, "It's the man who stands to his feet over and over who finally wins the battle!"

I was determined nothing would deter me now from making wildlife films. And, one day, soon, beautiful books would be published bearing my name, illustrated with my own photographs.

The First Books

THE NEXT HALF YEAR was tough to take. It proved to be one of those periods in life when it seemed all action stopped; all forward movement came to a standstill; and somehow any acute awareness of what I should do next was absent.

I was not mature enough in my understanding of God's ways to grasp the idea of waiting for His timing, waiting for His guidance, waiting for His Spirit to impress upon my spirit what His wishes were. I really knew nothing of resting in God—to repose on His utter reliability was foreign to me.

This was not because He had ever failed to touch my life in moments of special stress. He always had. But rather because of my energetic temperament, burning drive and fierce, hard will, I always precipitated the action, made the decisions and moved forcibly without always waiting for His approval.

Part of my dilemma was a letter that came from California, advising me that because of complicated changes in his financial affairs, the film producer could not go on with his project of world-wide wildlife films. So again I was thrown back in my tracks.

The government of British Columbia, having heard of my recent wildlife studies in Kenya, approached me to see if I would undertake similar work for them. But past experience with government bureaucracy and political people made me hesitant to become a civil servant.

Lastly, the general apathy of the local church, and its self-satisfied attitude of indifference to great causes really turned me off. I simply was not challenged by its self-centered activities to which so much time was devoted. I felt many of its functions were a farce, I wanted no part of its program at this point.

So, suddenly, running out of patience, eager to get something under way, I made several swift moves. In each of them it was essentially my will which was being asserted. Though I tried to convince myself my actions were guided by God, the truth was I was "taking the bit in my own teeth," ready to do "my own thing in my own way."

The gracious old home which I had purchased for mother years before was put on the auction block and sold hastily. This saved waiting for real estate agents to find a buyer. With the proceeds I purchased a derelict piece of coastal land that had been one of the very first pioneer farms on the west coast of the island. Its giant old barn had collapsed in a heap during a raging winter storm. The rail fences had rotted into the ground. The forest was invading the fields. But the beauty of its rock-ribbed mile of spectacular shoreline still remained unspoiled.

Like "Fairwinds" this property would demand enormous love, care, energy, work and expertise to turn it into a lovely oceanfront estate. We called it "Silver Spray Ranch" because of the foaming white spray thrown up by the great seas breaking against its rugged, rocky headlands.

The ranch house was restored and remodeled. Expert craftsmen and helpful friends provided the skill to do this thoroughly. So by the time winter settled in we were cozily ensconced in our new surroundings.

Though we were only about twenty-five miles further west along the coast than "Fairwinds," we soon discovered the climate was much more ferocious. Exposed to the full force of the open ocean we were battered by fierce westerly winds. Great banks of chill, gray fog enfolded us for days at a time. And the heavy rainfall made life a sodden, soggy ordeal much of the year.

Very quickly we realized that this had not been a wise move. Almost immediately the dampness and cold climate began to produce arthritic pains in my joints, back and spine.

These increased steadily over the next few years until they were so severe that some days I could not even rise from a couch, where I lay by the kitchen stove trying to keep warm. The crippling condition had me well-nigh immobilized.

Nonetheless, the long winter nights and quietness of our surroundings in the beautiful setting by the sea were conducive to writing and studying. So I dragged out the dog-eared African manuscript and spent months reworking it all with painstaking precision. From my slides I made up a collection of handsome photographs to illustrate the text. Also I was introduced to an aspiring young artist who agreed to furnish some exquisite pen and ink line drawings for the chapter headings.

Finally in an act of bold faith these were all carefully packaged up together and sent off to a publisher in London, England. Somehow I suspected that my rather British style of English might be better received there than in North America. I tried several publishers without success. Then the young artist came to me excitedly to say she had found out that the senior editor of Jarrolds was Cherry Kearton. His uncle, by the same name, had been one of Africa's great wildlife photojournalists. Perhaps my work would interest him.

We waited for months and months. No word came. As is so common, and often so maddening, there was only silence from the publishers. Still in flickering hope I clung to the old adage that "No news is good news."

Meanwhile I worked as hard as I could to establish a thriving livestock operation on the ranch. This time I was in a position to own both registered Shorthorn cattle and Cheviot sheep. But to my dismay I quickly discovered the land had been so leached out by the persistent Pacific storms that the soil was severely deficient in most of its trace minerals and nutrients. The cows and ewes delivered weak offspring barely able to survive on our sickly soil. So an intensive program of concentrated land improvement had to be initiated. Besides this, all new fences had to be built, more acres had to be cleared from the encroaching forest, and a new building erected to house livestock, feed and equipment as needed.

"Silver Spray Ranch" responded rapidly to the new management and attention it received. Quickly the fields and meadows running down to the shore began to grow lush and green with highly nutritious forage. The sheep and cattle began to flourish and revel in their contented country setting. The whole property took on that special aura of a place thriving in peace and beauty under proper care and management.

Then, one bleak, chill, blustery winter day I trudged out to the mailbox in big rubber boots and heavy wool mackinaw. My back was hunched against the driving rain. There was one forlorn, little, blue air-letter lying there alone. I looked at it half-interestedly. Suddenly I realized it was from half way round the world, in London.

Standing in the shelter of some nearby, moss-laden spruce trees, dripping with wetness, I tore the letter open with trembling fingers. It was from Cherry Kearton and the first lines read:

Dear Mr. Keller:
We have read your manuscript and examined your pictures. We like them very much. We are prepared to publish your work. . . . "Africa's Wild Glory. . . ."

It was as if 10,000 volts of electricity had shot through my entire nervous system. I was absolutely ecstatic, electrified with the news.

I dashed back to the house, my big boots pounding on the gravel road. I burst through the kitchen door, not even waiting to doff my wet bush jacket, waving the little blue letter wildly.

"Honey, honey!" I shouted excitedly to Phyllis. "It has happened, it has happened!"

We flung ourselves into each other's arms. We hugged, we kissed, we laughed, we cried, utterly consumed in joyous wonder by the good news from afar.

Eleven horrendous years of writing, writing, writing had finally earned their own rich reward. At last the final barrier had been breached. I had broken through into the ranks of recognized authors. I felt as though I stood ten feet tall. Now the dreams, the hopes, the longings of a lifetime would come to full fruition.

The gracious wind of God's Spirit had swept half-way around the world to do a wondrous work in the heart and mind of Cherry Kearton. He was to become my first editor, a dear friend, and a man near to my heart for nearly thirty years. Under his gracious, gentle guidance we would do at least six magnificent books together . . . books that were destined to capture wide international attention and high acclaim for their superb quality and fine content.

About nine months later, there lay in my hands a first copy of *Africa's Wild Glory*. It was a big book of well over 320 pages, printed on fine paper with numerous photographs to illustrate the text. Some were in black and white, others in color. The pen and ink sketches adorning the work gave it an extra dimension of artistic elegance.

These were the kind of books that had so enriched my own life as a young man. It was the caliber of writing that had shaped heroes for me to emulate and admire. Life had come full circle now to give me a sweet sense of genuine success and satisfaction.

With the publication of this first work there began to dawn upon my spirit two acute realizations. The first was the enormous power and influence of "the written word." Properly used it could convey messages of momentous import to multitudes of men and women all over the earth. It could be a tremendous force to mold opinions, move hearts, shape characters and inspire others to rich and lofty living. So under God's good hand it became a trust of great seriousness.

Secondly, it came home to me clearly that the gift of "writing," the ability to transmit ideas, thoughts and truth from one person to many others in this manner was a special responsibility from my Father. It was to be used, not to enhance my own ego, but to accomplish His purposes upon the planet.

For the next twenty-five years, the books that came from my pen (now some thirty of them), would be looked upon as joint efforts between God's guiding Spirit and myself. Always He has been regarded as the "Senior Partner" in the enterprise. Nor have I considered any success they enjoyed as much mine as His. It is He whom I have trusted to use the books to touch, inspire, bless and uplift others who read them. It is He who must be given the great credit for making them known now to millions of readers in various languages worldwide.

This is stated here in utter sincerity. Because I am a rather shy, reserved man who shuns publicity, it has been largely a case of the books becoming known through one reader telling another. Rarely indeed have I ever consented to engage in promotional schemes so often used to try and publicize one's work. It has always been my simple conviction that if the books are pleasing to God He will bless and multiply them. By the same measure, on my part, they should be of the highest quality and finest content possible—a credit both to me and to my Father.

The gathering and preparation of book material began to assume an ever-increasing role in my life. Of course the whole family was enthusiastic. There is an exciting and happy stimulus to hold in one's hands the final product that comes from months and years of steady toil, dedication and thought. Phyllis was delighted. The children were ecstatic.

Coupled with this were the letters which began to pour into our mailbox from readers in Great Britain, Canada, Australia, Malaya, South Africa and Kenya. More and more I became aware that I was regarded as a man who could convey to others a great concern for the conservation cause, which then was only just in its infancy.

Not only were readers aroused and stimulated by the message of those early books, but somehow they in turn were inspired to become actively engaged in the preservation of outdoor resources and the natural beauty of the biota. I was, without consciously trying to do so, becoming "a voice crying from the wilderness."

The net result was that I found more and more of my time taken up with mountain expeditions and photographic "safaris" in search of wildlife. Our location on the western shores of Vancouver Island was not the most central or convenient for such field work. So I began to consider the possibility of moving inland to the intermountain region where it would be easier and quicker to reach the major wilderness areas of the west.

Increasingly, too, I was becoming deeply concerned about the establishment of more national and provincial parks for the preservation of the wilds. In all of this enthusiasm, what I did not realize was that a steady but sure reversal of my own spiritual priorities was taking place again. Grizzly bears, mountain caribou, alpine meadows and virgin salmon streams were gradually usurping the place of prominence in my affairs. In themselves they were good and grand. But they were supplanting God in being the object of my first and greatest "love."

The Wilderness Years

Silver Spray Ranch had become a country estate of rare beauty and exquisite charm. Like "Fairwinds" it, too, lay secluded at the very end of a winding country road. Strangers would stand at the gate and gaze in quiet awe at the lovely rolling meadows that undulated down to the ocean edge. A few were daring enough to come in and request the pleasure of walking along the rugged shoreline. Others were too fearful of the magnificent, big bull that stood monarch in our herd of superb Shorthorns.

On sunny days the property was a paradise. But when fog, rain, snow and sleet swept over us from the Straits of Juan de Fuca it was a grim, gray realm of drilling dampness and cutting cold.

Finally, after long and careful deliberation, Phyllis and I decided to sell the ranch. Three main considerations constrained us to do this. The first was the increasing seriousness of my excruciating arthritic condition. During winter weather, especially, it well-nigh immobilized me. The second, mentioned in the previous chapter, was the advantage of moving into the mainland mountain region where great wilderness areas were close at hand.

The third and most decisive in the end was the ongoing education of Lynn and Rod. The little local school was fourteen miles away. The youngsters had to travel to and fro by bus. This meant leaving our door about 7:15 A.M. to trudge up the forested road to catch the bus, then riding it confined with children from half-breed homes, fishermen's floats, loggers' shacks and poor farm families. Traveling in the unhealthy and unwholesome atmosphere day after day was far from desirable—doubly so when some of their schoolmates were uncouth, foul-mouthed youths.

At best, bussing children long distances to school is a scheme to make use of modern transportation to reduce school costs. At worst, it is one of the great evils of the twentieth century foisted upon children. For in the close confinement of these contraptions, little ones are exposed to long and intimate contact with sometimes despicable companions.

For our two this was true. And when finally about 4:30 P.M., they would come tramping up the lane, often dripping wet in the rain, they had put in as long and trying a day as most adults do in the work force. Yet our son, when he started this dreadful schedule, was only seven years old.

So we decided to sell. For weeks there was little activity on the property. Then one spring morning the agent brought out a wealthy business magnate from Washington. He arrived attired in an immaculate pinstripe suit, shining black patent leather shoes and pure silk hose.

Immediately he demanded that we charter a pleasure boat for him, so he could cruise along the coast line and view the property from the sea. It was by far the easiest way for him to look it over.

I prevailed upon him to just walk across the acreage quietly with me. The promise that there would be steaming, home-baked buns and fresh coffee awaiting him when we got back finally induced him to go over the ranch on foot. Perhaps he feared our fierce-looking bull. But anyway we were gone quite a while.

Upon our return, he literally collapsed onto the couch in the kitchen. Lying there by the crackling wood stove fire he looked as pale as death. Finally the fresh buns and fragrant coffee restored his strength.

Tight-lipped, tough, abrasive, he made no commitment about the place. When he and the agent drove out of the gate I remarked to Phyllis: "Well—that's one city slicker who sure won't buy this outfit!"

To our unbounded astonishment he phoned long distance from Montana three days later. "Keller, I have decided to buy your property. I will be paying all cash on the condition I can retain its beautiful name—'Silver Spray Ranch.'" Of course he could!

So we made arrangements to move at summer's end, once the current crop of lambs and calves were marketed. Happily, the new owner agreed to take all the equipment and remaining stock. So it was a simple happy departure into wider ventures of wilderness life.

That summer I had made my first major expedition into the Rocky Mountain region. The photographic results had been absolutely phenomenal, exceeding my fondest hopes. So I was tremendously enthusiastic about establishing a home in the intermountain country. On my way back I stopped briefly in the beautiful Okanagan Valley.

This is the only area in Canada which boasts a true desert climate and terrain. Its summers are hot, clear, sunny. Cactus, greasewood and sagebrush abound. There are rattlesnakes and jack rabbits. Most important there is sufficient water from mountain streams and a lovely chain of sky blue lakes for irrigation. Here on the fertile desert benches, around the lakes, fine orchards flourish with apples, pears, peaches, apricots and cherries producing in abundance.

In a remarkable manner I stumbled across a unique old ranch of well over a thousand acres. It was for sale at a bargain price because the aged owner wished to move to town. It had an ancient log cabin that could be refurbished. With its shining lake, its singing stream, its wooded hills and open bunch grass slopes it would be a suitable base from which to work.

In fact, some seven books would be written within those rough log walls. We called it "Bear Claw Ranch" because there the bears came to den in winter. And there I would find fresh health.

In less than a year the arthritis had cleared up. The bright sunshine, dry climate and brisk atmosphere of the high country accomplished wonders for my condition. I was deeply grateful to God for not being further crippled by this debilitating disease.

With renewed vigor I now flung myself wholeheartedly

into serious, in-depth studies of North American wildlife. More than this, however, was the even broader view of the total wilderness world which I knew full well would be under siege in a few years from the rapacious onslaught of commerce, tourism, industry and modern man's technology. Time was against the wilds. I for one was determined to do my share to arouse public opinion for the preservation of irreplaceable areas of pristine splendor.

The preface to my second book, *Canada's Wild Glory*, will convey unmistakably to the reader the zeal, energy and the enthusiasm with which I poured out my life in this cause.

"The whispering of forests under wind; the high faint cries of birds of wing; the murmur of sand and rocks under water; these are voices seldom heard in our radio broadcasts, schoolrooms, or television programmes. The bugling of elk in a wild glade, the thundering heads of 'bighorns' in battle, are sounds not heard beyond the rock ridges of their realm— never heard in the carpeted halls of our council chambers. The dancing hordes of wild flowers that fling themselves in cascades of colour across the alpine slopes seldom find reflection in the drab laws of the land. The majestic appeal of a mountain, that tugs at the heart of even the most callous human in its presence, makes few motions in Parliament.

"That is why some of us who are fellow to the wilds feel compelled, in spite of ourselves, to shout aloud for them. Yesterday, today, and tomorrow we must continually be reminded of the priceless wilderness heritage entrusted to our care. That is the theme which runs through this work. It is an attempt, both in words and photographs, to portray a fragment of the 'Wild Glory' that I have known and loved.

"This book makes no pretence at being a profound reference work on Canadian wildlife. It is, rather, an honest attempt to share with the reader, some of the exhilaration, thrust, and thrill of life in the vigorous 'back country' of this continent. My genuine hope is that a little of the enthusiasm and inspiration which wild things and wilderness areas have poured into my life will spill over to those who read and perhaps encourage them to set out and taste further for themselves.

"Somehow this generation must rediscover that the human

heart can be lifted by free birds in flight; that the soul can draw strength from the noble solitude of mountain ramparts; that the mind can be refreshed with the untarnished beauty of an alpine meadow; that the body can gain vigour from the challenge of the trail and life under open skies.

"It is for us all to remember that the earth does not belong to us. We belong to it. At best we are entrusted with a few brief years of life in which to relish the splendours about us. We are but an infinitesimal fragment of a staggering universe. It behooves us to cherish well those natural glories entrusted to our care. The humble knowledge that we have no claim upon them other than the honour of passing them on in at least as fine a form as we found them should lend honest dignity to our efforts on their behalf."

I found no challenge of the high country too tough to tackle. With pack on back and cameras in hand I hiked into remote wilderness areas, where, in those days, another man's footprint may not have trodden for ten years. I broke into new terrain, camped in shining alpine meadows, lingered beside remote glacier lakes more lovely than words can portray on paper.

I spent hours, days, weeks with Rocky Mountain bighorns, Olympic elk, grizzly and black bears, mountain goats, Mule deer, White Tail deer, coyotes, beaver and other smaller species of wildlife. They all became my friends of hoof, wing and claw.

Because they could not speak for themselves I undertook to be their voice shouting from the wilds. With utter abandon I accepted every invitation that came my way to address wildlife associations, national natural history societies, service clubs or church groups. Often these lectures were illustrated with a series of superb Kodachrome slides, arranged with meticulous care, to present their own moving chronicle of resource conservation.

I pled with members of Parliament, with officials who formulated government policy, even with the Provincial Premier and others in positions of influence, to take the steps necessary to set aside wilderness areas for posterity. My pleas were not in vain. For in due course The Cathedral Lakes Park in the interior came into being, as did also The Pacific Rim Park on the West Coast.

Public opinion, too, began to be aroused. A giant ground swell of wide interest in resource conservation began to move across the West. Young people in particular became keen on camping, hiking and outdoor recreation. The enthusiasm for preservation of natural beauty, native flora and fauna was wonderful to observe.

In a special, private way I sensed that in all of this my life was being poured out, spilled out as an offering, in sacrifice for the wilderness I loved so intensely. People often asked, "Phillip, how can you endure such hardships in the field, go to such lengths in the mountains, without becoming discouraged?" My prompt reply simply was, "When you are in love with your work, obstacles are no deterrent—only a challenge to greater things."

During these "wilderness years" an adventuresome dimension of achievement, of success, of fulfilled dreams, of high hopes come true, enriched my days. Often as I sat alone on a high ridge scanning far horizons I marveled how gracious and generous God had been to grant me such exhilarating episodes.

Few, few men had been so favored.

Perhaps even more important, however, was a strange, quiet inner awareness that my heavenly Father was waiting patiently for my priorities to be turned around. It was He who had arranged, brought into being and sustained the biota. Yet I was more enthralled with it than with Him. Mountains and streams, forests and flower fields, big game and surging storms took precedence over the One who endowed me with the capacity to enjoy them.

As I entered my early forties an unusual unease began to stir within my spirit. All alone by some wilderness campfire, or high on a wind-lashed ridge with mountain ranges stretching to the far skyline, I became aware that somehow I was "missing the mark" in life. In taking serious stock of my exciting careers I was made conscious by God's gracious Spirit that a man's life did not consist in the abundance of his possessions—even if they were exhilarating experiences, signal successes by the world's standards, or even dreams come true.

There was more than all of this.

Much more!

And that was to intimately know and love the Lord God

Himself. It was to come to that position in personal contact with him where the wind of His Spirit was just as vital to the life of my spirit, as was the clean, sharp wind off the glaciers: life—vigorous life—to my lungs.

Always, for as long as I could recall from early boyhood, there had been a craving to know Christ. But in midlife this craving became more intense, more demanding, compelling, urgent like a yearning, burning quest for God's very person and presence.

He had allowed me to try and taste, yes even triumph in endeavors of every kind. Yet none, no matter how grand or worthwhile, had fully satisfied this strange, strong longing of my soul. Success in many forms, in various arenas of life, once achieved, still left me with an inner unquenched thirst which only He could satisfy.

So it was I determined, somehow, to search for Him with all my soul and spirit. In reality it was the wind of His Spirit who played upon my heartstrings with such strong persistence.

Three Hills

RUNNING PARALLEL WITH all my wilderness work was the challenge of bringing "Bear Claw Ranch" into shape. Like so many mountain ranches it had suffered sadly at the hands of those who had tried to wrest a living from its wild and tumbled terrain.

Erosion, overgrazing, excessive timber-cutting, ghastly gullies, weed-infested fields and dying water sources were all part of the pathetic picture. It would take several years of skillful management and loving care to turn things around on this thousand acres of grand, high country.

The stimulating success of our efforts has been told with moving earnestness in the book, *Under Desert Skies*. With energy and enthusiasm the log cabin, perched in a grassy glade above the lake, was restored to usefulness. From its open windows one could look in every direction and see only the wild upland world of sagebrush hills, timbered ridges and rugged cliffs of the desert.

It was here the red-tailed hawks soared and cried on the warm, rising thermals. Here the deer came to feed on the pungent watercress by the springs. Here the bears foraged for berries in the timbered gullies. Here the coyotes called from the coulee rim under full moonlight.

It was a world of burning heat in summer, of bitter cold in winter, but of breathless beauty in spring and fall. Then the fresh green grass and desert wild flowers adorned the range. And, under cloudless Indian summer skies the sumac burned fiery red while the birches glowed gold.

Here Rod and Lynn roamed free as the mountain winds. They camped under canvas. They swam in the lake. They fished for trout in the sparkling stream. They sat beside a hundred campfires.

But again, as at "Silver Spray Ranch," the question of quality schooling and higher education became a burning issue. Our land was surrounded on two sides by a magnificent region of upland ranges which belonged to the local native Indian band. They became dear friends and courteous neighbors. Yet their youngsters had limited aspirations. Some were satisfied to be top rodeo riders or high-line loggers, but nothing beyond that.

Phyllis and I made a point of praying seriously about the matter of schooling. In His own generous way our Father led us to visit friends at Three Hills, Alberta. This little community, perched out on the windswept, open prairies, lies within distant view of the Rockies. It is famous, world-wide, for its splendid Prairie Bible Institute. From this Christian center sturdy, fearless missionaries have been sent out to scores of countries all over the earth. To thousands it is known affectionately as "Prairie."

Combined with the Bible institute itself was both a Christian high school and grade school. These were properly accredited with the Alberta government. They carried excellent high quality curriculums. The teachers were earnest Christians. And, most important, God's Word was given a place of prominence in the life of the students.

We decided the finest contribution we could make to our children was to establish a home there. It would mean extra travel for me to go back and forth both to the ranch and to the mountains. But I was willing to endure this as long as the youngsters could grow up in an atmosphere of godly devotion and Christian enthusiasm.

Little did I then realize that, not only would they benefit, but so also would I, in ways utterly unknown. It was my Father's skillful arrangement for maneuvering me into the place of His appointment. "Prairie" would become another pivot point in my career.

By this time in my life I was into my early forties. During times of quiet reflection, alone in the mountains, or ensconced in my remote cabin, I came to see clearly that I was a man of divided loyalties, divided interests, divided ambitions. It is difficult to portray on paper the peculiar pain of one "split" by counteracting tugs and pulls in life. But I must try, for it is the rock-bottom dilemma facing thousands of Christians trapped in a tormenting "wilderness experience" in their walk with God—a life style in which they are going nowhere with God, simply moving in circles of selfish self-centeredness.

On the one hand it seemed so obvious I was "riding high" in terms of adventure and achievement. The beautiful books bearing my name were bringing wide recognition. With the royalties I could undertake more and more extensive mountain expeditions. My wildlife studies and big-game photography provided heart-pounding excitement in the grandeur of remote wilderness areas. I was producing some remarkable films on the life habits of big game. The ranch was flourishing. My family were reveling in their new surroundings at Three Hills.

On the surface all seemed to be so successful, so well assured, so stimulating.

But on the other hand I sensed a bleak barrenness within my spirit—as bare as a bleached, cast-off buck horn lying dry and dead on a shale slope in the sun. The Spirit of the Living God was present with me, yet, always standing, as it were, at arm's length from me: close at hand, it is true, but somehow strangely just out of reach, out of intimate touch.

It was Phyllis, who, from time to time, in her quiet, gentle, understanding way would remark to me, "Darling, you have such terrific drive and enthusiasm for the wilds; for mountains; for the ranch; for conservation." Then she would smile softly and pause a moment. "But you really don't seem to care that much about people or their problems. God loves them, too, you know."

She was never one to berate or belittle me. She was too loyal, too faithful a friend, too wise a woman ever to try to make her man into a mouse. Instead with her keen intelligent understanding, her lovely charm, her sincere praise, she made me walk ten feet tall. But God's Spirit used her gentle remarks from time to time, like polished mirrors, to make me see myself as I really was.

And what I saw I began to abhor. My tough, hard-headed,

strong-willed, self-centered determination to succeed and surpass had precluded giving Christ complete control of either my career or my character. He was there, but only as an advisor or associate one turned to in time of stress or need. He did not govern my choices. He did not decide my deliberations. He did not command my career. He did not actually initiate or energize my enterprises.

In a sentence—I lived and worked and planned for Phillip Keller. Yet in that strange dichotomy so typical of thousands of Christians, I claimed I lived for Christ. I was caught betwixt the viselike jaws of sincerity and self-deception. How, how, could I ever break loose out of such a constricted condition?

One of my first serious attempts was to undertake a biographical book on The Shantymen Missionaries of the West Coast. These were the rugged, sturdy, selfless fellows who first came ashore to our seaside cottage at "Fairwinds." Their joyous enthusiasm in God's work, their total self-giving to help others in lonely places, had partially inspired me to go to the Masai in Kenya.

Perhaps by spending weeks on their boat, *Messenger II,* and long hours in their company, I could or would come to a clearer understanding of what it means to truly know God. It proved to be a most profitable experience. It aroused within my spirit an even more intense desire to love Christ and commune with Him as they did.

The missionary biography, *Splendor from the Sea,* which emerged from that interlude with the "Shanty Boys" was an instant success. It was my first venture into Christian writing that opened up a whole new world of endeavor.

The work was beautifully illustrated with photographs, some of which I took. Others came from professional photographers who had done a story on the mission for *Life* magazine. It also bore exquisite line drawings executed by a dear woman who had spent long, lonely years as a lighthouse keeper's wife on the rugged west coast.

One of her life-long dreams had been to use her talent to do something beautiful for God. When I invited her to prepare the sketches for *Splendor from the Sea* she was ecstatic. Just before the book was released to the public, I went to visit her. She had been stricken with a most malignant cancer. She lay weak and dying. Yet amid her agony and pain she held my hands in hers and whispered in my ear: "Phillip, our Father is so faithful! He has spared me to see my work and talent used to His honor!"

A few days later she was gone . . . to glory.

But in the stillness of that sick room, God's Spirit had spoken to me in thundering tones heard by no other human ears. The stabbing, searching, searing question had come home to my innermost will—"Is my work, my time, my talent being used to honor God—or just me?"

Steadily, surely the wondrous wind of God's Spirit was pressing upon my spirit. He was bringing me to that pivot point in life where one must decide either to step out and live wholeheartedly for God in fearless faith, or turn back to tramp the tired old trails of self-gratification and selfish self-interest.

But, how? How could this happen in a personality as head-strong as mine? How could such a capitulation to the control of Christ come in a will tough as tungsten steel, such as I owned?

Between my exhilarating mountain trips, wildlife studies, writing books, giving conservation lectures, and development of the ranch I tried to squeeze in time for some of the services and speakers at Prairie Bible Institute. The school was fortu-nate to have great men and women of God from all over the world come to the campus for conferences, conventions and special student sessions.

So I began to be exposed to some of the finest expository preaching and teaching to be found anywhere. More than this, new friendships were formed with devout staff members on campus. Their single-minded devotion and total dedica-tion to the Lord moved me mightily. I saw in their joyous self-sacrifice a living, practical demonstration of what it meant to lay down one's life for others . . . no matter what the cost.

But it was partially this cost of following Christ, this "price to pay" in gracious self-giving and self-sacrifice for the sake of others, that daunted me. I really was not yet ready totally to subject my will to the government of God. I was not fully prepared to capitulate yet to the claims of Christ for control of my affairs. I was not at all sure I could submit myself to the supreme sovereignty of the Spirit of the living God.

I was too tough a man.

I had driven myself to the ultimate in order to succeed.

I had hardened my will until like a shaft of steel nothing could bend or break or bind it. It was mine to do with as I wished—or so I assumed (*wrongly*).

No one would lord it over me. No one would dictate to me. No one would lead me about or push me around. I was my own free will spirit determined to fulfill my own desires.

So in essence it became a deadly stand-off between God and me. Looking back in retrospect to those months, twenty years ago, I marvel at the patience of God with one so petulant and perverse.

Mentally my conscious desire was to be God's man.

Emotionally all my longings were to love Christ and serve Him.

But volitionally, my will had not yet submitted unequivocally to God's Spirit.

Mr. L. E. Maxwell, president and founder of Prairie, having become a dear and respected friend, with his profound insight, named me "The Maverick"—the untamed, unroped colt upon which no one had ever stamped his brand of ownership. It was a true and appropriate description.

Yet the irony of the situation was that at the school I could see the damage done in the lives of students, who, like myself, were "mavericks." I could see the folly of flaunting God's authority. I could discern those who became derelicts because they refused to come under the divine discipline of God's Word. I could understand the utter emptiness of lives barren and wasted because they flung off the yoke of obedience and respect for God's Spirit.

In His own persistent, patient forbearance God began to give me an insatiable thirst for His Word. I found myself, for the first time in my life, spending hours and hours searching the Scriptures, poring over its pages, exposing myself to its truth.

One of the major emphases at the Institute was the principle of each person seeking for himself to find God's wishes revealed in the Word. It was constantly reiterated that the person who sought God in His Word, would indeed find illumination there by God's own Spirit. Scripture was compared with Scripture. And the Spirit of Christ became the ultimate "teacher" who would lead one into all truth, taking the things of Christ and transmitting them to man in wondrous, living reality.

A crucial, burning issue which God's Word revealed to me at this stage of my spiritual saga was the whole matter of forgiveness. Never before had I realized the titanic cost of suffering borne by Christ at Calvary, in order to extend perfect pardon and full forgiveness to me as a man. It was His impeccable life, poured out in total self-giving on my behalf and in my stead, which atoned for all my willful waywardness and wrong-doing.

Such stupendous self-sacrifice to save me humbled my spirit, pulverized my pride and made me acutely aware of the great debt of gratitude I owed my God.

This acute awareness of my Father's forgiveness then constrained me to make right the wrong, vindictive attitude I held against those who had wronged me. I had to go to those who had injured me so deeply when "Fairwinds" was taken as a military base. I had to write to those who had been so unfair to mother after dad's death. I had to clear up unforgiven grudges with those who had double-crossed me in business.

This was not an easy road. It called for self-humiliation. It called for utter honesty. It called for cleansing of conscience. But it brought peace, inner light and exquisite liberty of spirit.

The Pivot Point

IT HAD BEEN ONE of those still, serene Indian summer interludes in the northern Rockies. The days were bright, sharp,
stimulating to the senses, invigorating to the soul. New-fallen
snow dusted the peaks in immaculate whiteness. The lower
slopes were aglow with the autumn tones of burnt-orange,
gold and rust from grass tinted with frost.

Through this breathless, quiet, upland region I had stalked
the great herds of Rocky Mountain elk in their majestic migrations. I had photographed the Bighorn sheep in their rock-
girt realm. I had watched the wide sweep of Golden eagles
soaring above the crags on their outstretched wings.

It had been a superb season! Now I was heading home
for Three Hills. Somehow my entire being was charged with
vigor, with achievement, with the zest of the high country.
But also, strangely, I was anxious to attend the fall Keswick
Convention at the Institute.

A day or so before it began I said to Phyllis, "I have made
up my mind to attend every meeting, take part in every session and participate in all the prayer times. This is the teaching dad and mother loved so much."

Whether or not I had a clear comprehension that I was
approaching the pivot point in my walk with God is not certain. What I do know is that a burning, yearning desire to
truly come to love God, as I loved the wondrous wilderness
world He created, engulfed me. There were times in the

mountains when their majestic beauty, their stimulating scenery, the cool clean air off the heights were a heady wine to me. So I sensed deep in my spirit that in the same way a man filled, swept up in and stimulated by the wondrous wind of God's Spirit would be likewise exultant, charged with a divine dynamic.

For four full days I attended every session at the Institute. Finally I could not stand another service. I needed to be alone. I needed to be absolutely still before God. I needed, not more sermons, songs and seminars, but the still small voice of God's own presence speaking to me.

Moses had his "burning bush" in the desert. Gideon had his "oak tree" by the winepress. Elijah had his "cave in the rock" high on a mountain. And I had my "high cliffs" overlooking a crystal stream that cascaded out of the foothills.

There I went, absolutely alone, determined that I would hear from God in a way never experienced before. For hours I paced back and forth atop the cliffs, tears coursing down my cheeks, in agony of earnestness, beseeching Christ to make Himself very real to me.

It was a man hungry, thirsty, longing for the Lord who cried aloud from those cliff tops. "Oh, God," I pleaded from the depths of my spirit. "You told us, 'Blessed are they who hunger and thirst after righteousness, for they shall be filled!' " I raised my arms in anguish of supplication, "Come now, move into my spirit, fill my life, my entire being with Yourself, just as this stream from the glaciers flows into this valley before me!"

Then there came the quiet, gentle response of God's voice: "My Spirit is imparted in plenitude to the one prepared to obey me. Your love for me is demonstrated, not by emotion, but by your readiness to comply with My wishes; to do My will. Are you ready to give me your will?" There was total silence. I was astonished, taken aback at the apparent simplicity of the straightforward exchange extended to me.

I would give Him my will (my heart).

He would give me Himself.

In utter brokenness, compounded of joy, light relief and surging gratitude I fell to my knees on the wild sod and there bowed myself before my God.

"Father, from this hour, with Your presence and Your

power, I undertake to do whatever You ask; to go wherever
You wish; to be whoever You desire." The words spoken
audibly came in clear articulation, "I am totally available to
Your purposes for me upon the planet."

It was a compact of tremendous import. It was the pivot
point in my walk with God. I had crossed the "great divide"
into a new region of personal, intimate contact with Christ.

There was no ecstatic sensation. Rather, there enveloped
the whole of my being, body, mind, emotions, will and spirit
an acute awareness of God's gracious, wondrous Presence.
He was with me, in me, to empower, to direct, to abide
throughout the rest of life.

In calm repose and supreme peace I went home.

Phyllis, in her cheerful, happy way met me at the door. I
had been gone all day. "Darling!" she ejaculated, surprised
and taken aback, "You are utterly radiant! What has happened?"

It was weeks before I felt free to tell her even a small
part of all that took place that day. For it had been a sacred
interlude shared by a common man alone with God's Spirit.
But from that hour the entire tenor and direction of my
life began to change dramatically.

All sorts of people who had known me before would stop
me and remark: "You seem so different now. What has happened? What did you do? How did God touch you?"

As a simple, searching lay person there was little I could
say. "Just obey Him, and He will move into your life. Resist
Him and He won't!"

My favorite verse during those days became: *"For it is God
who worketh in you, both to will* and *to do* of his good pleasure"
(Phil. 2:13).

At last, at long last, I had been converted in the realm
of my will. No longer did I evade God's hands. He was free
now to work out His good purposes in my affairs.

To put it in rough ranch language: My Master, at last,
had flung His lariat of love around me. And now I bore
His brand.

Unlike so many Christian biographies where people tell
about the dreadful disasters that overtook them before they
capitulated to Christ, my story at this point seemed just the
opposite. Where others recount the trauma of fragmented

families, criminal records, financial disasters, shattered health or perhaps addiction to drugs or alcohol that drove them to seek God, there was in my case a totally different perspective.

I was at the pinnacle of prowess in my various professions. By this time I was an author of international recognition. My outdoor photography had attracted wide acclaim. I was regarded as a leading advocate in the burgeoning conservation movement. I had earned an enviable reputation as a field naturalist. My ranches had become show places. I enjoyed a wide circle of friends. And my children were progressing splendidly in their studies.

It was not wreckage and disaster that I was turning over to the government of God. It was not something despicable of which I was divesting myself (except my stubborn will). It was not confusion and chaos I was leaving. Rather it was "success" by the world's standards, which I was called upon to set aside now, in order to fully follow my Master.

Step by step there would be a painful path to tread in taking up the cross that cut across all my own aims and ambitions in order to do God's will. My priorities would have to be reversed. In the process there would be struggle, suffering and sorrow. But with it all would come boundless new benefits and adventures with God to equal anything in the high country.

Because so much of this was so private, and so personal, there is no intention to elaborate on the events here. Only the highlights will be mentioned in order that the reader understand clearly how a new foundation had to be laid in my life for future service.

Nor should it be construed that others will be dealt with by God as I was. His Spirit leads each of us along a special, unique path of His own preparation.

One of the first major areas of my life upon which God laid His hand was my love for the land. This instinct for enjoying and living in a country setting had always been a profound part of my life. Good soil, choice livestock, long vistas, wide skies, the fierce freedom of "being boss" on one's own domain, were a powerful force in my make-up.

I had come from a family where owning land and developing it for high productivity was a surging stimulus—not only because of the intrinsic beauty of a well-managed estate, but also because of the security it offered.

At "Bear Claw Ranch," especially, we had ample land, abundant water from the streams and springs, plenty of timber and excellent resources to provide for our future.

Now the Spirit of the Lord began to make me aware that my resources, my security, my confidence should repose in God, my Father, not in my real estate holdings.

One would assume I should have learned this lesson well in the loss of "Fairwinds." But some of us are slow indeed to grasp the great eternal principles of God. I am one!

Increasingly the inner conviction came upon me that I should part with the ranch. Not just dispose of it, but actually give it away freely to those more needy than myself who were actively serving God.

This was a tough request to comply with heartily. At first I was disposed to debate the issue with Christ. How would I properly provide for my family? What about the extra costs of special Christian schooling? Where would we go to live when they went on to advanced studies?

The age-old, eternal question came to me as it did to Peter by the lake. The Master asked, "Do you love Me more than these?—these acres, streams, lake, hills and rolling range?"

Finally one day, sitting by the lake, utterly alone before the Lord, I completely capitulated. "Father, just as You wish, I give it all, gladly!!"

Almost overnight, after this decision was made, requests began to come in to me for feature articles, a regular magazine column, and photographs from editors I never had met. My income, instead of diminishing from the disposal of the ranch, had begun to escalate. God was simply showing me in unmistakable ways that He could easily care for all our needs.

But even more important, though I knew it not at the time, I was being freed up to go and serve in city centers where God had work for me to do. Burdened with the ranch responsibilities I would not have been available to these new purposes arranged by God.

The next arena of my life to be touched by God's Spirit was the wilderness world I loved so intensely. The wilds had always provided me with enormous pleasure. I am essentially a son of the wild places. I am "at home" there, at ease, relaxed, contented in the company of trees, hills, mountains and wildlife. I am not a sophisticated offspring of our twentieth-century civilization. In fact I look upon our superficial society with a certain sense of disdain and disgust for its corrupt culture, its brazen ballyhoo, its false façade, its deceptive duplicity . . . all of which have tainted my life.

But God was calling me persistently to disengage myself from the wilderness. He was asking me to set aside the solitude, the seclusion and quiet serenity of my beloved mountains, rivers and plains. Instead He was now calling me to enter fully into the mainstream of our mad, modern world of the urban environment. There I would be finding my days filled with the burdens of broken hearts, broken homes, broken hopes, broken people.

This was not an easy transition for a man who reveled in remote places, who loved the gentle tempo of the high country, who thrived on vigorous outdoor adventures.

But I had made a compact with Christ on those high cliffs. If He wanted me constricted and cramped in a city setting, I was prepared to go into the "concrete jungle." It would be a crushing, bruising adjustment, but it was His way to have my life become broken bread and poured out wine for the benefit of others.

Bit by bit, in stern reality and real-life situations, I was being shown what the Master meant when He said "That unless a seed be buried and undergo dissimulation, it could never germinate into a fruitful, reproductive plant." So He would plant me in the soil of new situations and strange people where my life would have to be literally laid down that others might live.

It is no easy, simple thing to become the Master's man! There is a cross to carry. And that cross is the powerful principle of putting aside all one's own special interests and private preferences, to go out and do whatever God demands . . . asking no questions.

The third painful parting, and one which there is no intention of dramatizing here, was a willingness to give up Phyllis.

We had now been married for over twenty years. She had been a remarkable life companion. Her gracious spirit, her noble character, her strong, serene faith in Christ, her sweet disposition had all been an inspiration and strength to me during our years of adventure together.

She was stricken again with the sinister scourge of the most virulent cancer known to science. Soon she would be taken from me. In fact it would be on the very day of our twenty-third anniversary that she would be swept away through the portal of death to enter the realm of eternal rest with her Lord.

This was not an easy parting.

So amid all the death to self that was endured, I could understand ever more clearly the costly path of pain my parents had trod in Africa, that others might live.

This is ever God's way. For out of death springs new life. Through laid-down lives emerges God's divine energy to quicken others.

In the years ahead, in His own good time, in His own special way, God would arrange for another lovely lady to share our great new adventures together. For He is not only the God of all consolation and comfort to His people, but He is also the God of wondrous compensation in our losses.

Ursula with her vivacious personality, her strong courage, her shining spirit would become my cheerful companion. Together we would face the future with fortitude. Quietly, calmly we would rejoice in the wonder of the way in which God's Spirit would lead us gently into ever widening fields of service.

Wider Horizons

REFLECTING BACK upon those crucial years following my cliff-top encounter with Christ, I marvel at His mercy, generosity and faithfulness to me. It was as though He took me strongly by the hand to lead step by step into ever broadening areas of service. He set before me by His Spirit ever wider horizons of adventure with Himself. There was a stimulating awareness of His presence to face the most formidable challenges.

In ways which I do not understand, even to this day, invitations began to come in for me to speak to groups of students or young people in churches. What was I to say? Who was I to speak? What credentials did I have?

The basic fact is that once a person is totally open and available to the purposes of God, He prepares a people to receive the Word from that individual. It is not that God is waiting for "perfect" people to declare His truth—only that He will use the one ready to do His bidding and carry out His will. The chief credential for the Master's service is not technical training or weighty theology, but a broken and contrite spirit through which His Spirit can move and speak.

At first, as a very ordinary lay person, this daunted me a bit. I had no diplomas or degrees of divinity from any Bible school or seminary. I was simply a rough-hewn mountain man. My long years in other careers were, it seemed, scarcely suited to one now called upon to stand before audiences to speak for God.

Some apprehension, a certain overwhelming sense of enormous responsibility both to God and men, and a genuine feeling of unworthiness pervaded all my preparations to speak to others on eternal issues.

Where before, boldly, fearlessly I addressed audiences about resource conservation or wildlife preservation, now I was cast in another rôle . . . that of spokesman for the living Lord. This was a most solemn assignment that sometimes well-nigh made, and still does make, me tremble.

It was a case of dying a thousand deaths to deliver God's Word in sincerity, urgency and integrity.

For every minute I spoke, it seemed an hour had to be spent in study, prayer, meditation and stillness before the Lord. My earnest petition always has been, "Oh, God, give me Your message. And then, Father, give me the courage to deliver that message."

For so many years I had searched for and longed to really know Christ, that when I now spoke to others about Him my burning desire was that He should become to them a living, present "Friend." That they should find Him to be the faithful One who could bring enormous purpose and direction into their lives. That He, by His Spirit, could enable them to live lofty, noble lives of strength and serenity amid a sordid society . . . no matter what their past had been.

Because of this view I could find no place for levity, flamboyancy or showmanship in speaking for God. I was not standing before men to entertain them. I was not there to win their applause or gain popularity. I was there as one who in utmost sincerity and childlike simplicity endeavored to pass on life-changing principles to perishing people.

Often I used simple, basic parables drawn from my long years on the land or in the mountains. It was the approach Jesus had used. God's Spirit anointed the messages to convey His truth with great clarity. Often listeners remarked to me years later that they could readily recall the practical talks I had shared with them so long before.

For this I have always been heartily grateful to God. And it is indeed humbling to realize how He deigns to use the lowly things of life to perform His majestic work in the lives of His people. To be a part of His purposes has always been a high and wondrous honor.

In this way I began to be made aware that the particular gift of God's gracious Spirit given to me was essentially that of a teacher. My increasing emphasis was the practical application of spiritual truth to people's lives so that they could learn to walk with God by faith and please Him forever. I was not a brilliant orator. I was not an impassioned, flaming evangelist, though people came to know and love Christ. I was not a miracle-worker. My rôle was teaching truth in quiet earnestness. In this way God drew souls to Himself.

In due course, along with addressing a wide variety of churches, youth groups, retreats and conventions, an opportunity was presented to serve as a lay pastor in a community church.

These openings were not my arrangements. I did not seek them. They were simply the work of God. For that basic reason I never looked upon them as "my work." I always reminded my colleagues that—"This is God's work—this is His church—these are His people—this is His interest, as much as ours—we are simply co-workers with Him."

In all of these endeavors it moved me deeply to see the continuous love, compassion and faithfulness of the Lord in touching the lives of listeners. To see men and women turn from darkness to light, from despair to love, from death to life in Christ is tremendously thrilling. It is deeply rewarding for all the agony and anguish of travail in seeing others come to a new birth in God by His Spirit.

Steadily but surely more and more of my time was taken up with teaching Bible study groups. I soon found that there was an enormous hunger for God's Word in many hearts. Where most churches can hardly get a dozen people to mid-week services, these classes filled up with eager people.

I was especially keen to reach men. Women were encouraged to bring their husbands, boy friends or brothers. The upshot was that businessmen, professional people and retired executives were coming to find Christ—to understand His Word and to live for Him.

People from all denominations were drawn to these classes. Word went around that for many the Bible became a "Living Book" through which God revealed Himself clearly by His Spirit. In all of this I was genuinely glad.

In the field of writing my endeavors moved more and more

into the preparation of devotional books. It was often at the special request of those who had shared in the Bible studies that these truths were put into manuscript form. The conviction grew strongly among many, many people that such books could be used by God's Spirit to inspire and enrich His people all over the world.

Somehow, much to my dismay, Christian publishers were not always as enthusiastic. Some of the manuscripts went from publisher to publisher to publisher with nothing but rejection following rejection. It takes a tough and tenacious temperament to keep trying to find an editor who will agree to produce one's work after being told over and over it simply is not suitable.

A quiet, deep, settled conviction lay always upon my spirit, that if the publishers would just produce the books, God Himself would bless them. It was He who would use them to touch lives at great depths and turn seeking souls to Himself. It was He who would anoint these humble volumes to inspire, lift, heal and cheer His children the world around.

And this He has done now in many languages, to millions upon millions of readers all across the earth.

I take no personal credit for this. It is the work of the Lord. Consistently I have refused to participate in publicity campaigns, promotional schemes or autograph parties. It has always been my contention that an author should produce work of such high caliber that it bears sufficient intrinsic worth to stand on its own merit. Thus, when it is pleasing to God, He in turn will be pleased to bless it in thousands of hearts and homes at His own great pleasure.

As the books became known, writing and photographic assignments came in to visit missionaries in various countries. Eventually I met with over 300 in 30 countries.

It would be a great adventure to see God at work in places as remote as the jungles of Malaya, the wind-chilled mountain passes of Pakistan or the sun-burdened deserts of the Sahara. In great university cities, in country villages, amid the most primitive bamboo huts I would sense the Spirit of Christ calling out a chosen people for Himself. From the ranks of scholars, professional people, urban-dwellers, country peasants and jungle tribesmen Christ was preparing a special, beloved bride, His church, for Himself.

In many of these places, among all sorts of people, it was a joy to speak for My Master. It was likewise a heart-thrilling encouragement to observe the profound dedication and generous sacrifice of men and women the world over willing to lay down their lives that others might receive the great Good News of our Father's love for them in Christ.

An exciting little episode on one of these assignments will help the reader to appreciate how gracious God was to me.

My itinerary called for travel from Karachi, Pakistan to Aden, Arabia, then on to Addis Ababa in Ethiopia, and from there across the continent to Lagos in Nigeria. To my dismay it had not been possible to schedule a flight into Kenya, though I longed to see the land I loved so dearly after an absence of nearly ten years.

As we flew in over Aden a fierce desert dust storm suddenly blew up. Immediately the pilot came on the loudspeaker and announced that he was not cleared to land, so his only alternative was to divert the flight to Kenya. I burst out laughing with joy. My Father could rearrange schedules with ease and in a hurry.

The airline apologized profusely and put me up at the finest hotel in Nairobi. They were sorry it would be three days before another flight could take me on to my proper destination.

But I was exactly where God wanted me. Within an hour I found that one of my most esteemed Masai friends for whom I had prayed for nine years was ensconced in a fine office only a few blocks away. He had been elevated to general secretary of The British and Foreign Bible Society for all East Africa. What a reunion we had! He told me of the spiritual awakening among the Masai!

That evening I was invited to a friend's home where many of my former associates in the country were gathering for a festive celebration. They had come from all over Kenya and Tanzania. The Lord had arranged for me to be there, too, all the way from Canada. What a celebration! What rekindling of old acquaintances! What a joy in the Lord!

The last day before my departure, a truck was put at my disposal so I could drive out into some of my beloved Masai country. There, in the sweeping expanses of the lion-colored plains, I spent several hours alone in quiet company with some of my wild friends.

In His own special, intimate, precious way God's Spirit showed me again how carefully He was guiding my life, arranging my affairs with great adventures and keen delights.

Of these, perhaps one of the most rewarding was the remarkable way in which the wildlife films I had made in the mountains were televised across the nation from coast to coast. It turned out to be one of those "beautiful bonuses" which our Father loves to bestow upon His own.

Somehow, the Canadian Broadcasting Corporation heard about my big game studies. So I was invited to their west coast studios in Vancouver for an initial viewing.

The C.B.C. staff were tremendously enthusiastic. They immediately requested the rights to the material. It was made clear to me that because of government policy, no opportunity would be given for Christian witness in the series. Still I believed God could use them to touch the lives of viewers. And He did. For subsequently mail came in from across the nation telling of souls deeply stirred by the majestic footage . . . displaying God's glory everywhere.

Most important the chief director called me aside privately one day. "Phillip," he said, looking into my eyes, "we get all sorts of sordid types in these studios. But, you have come in here like a fresh wind, blowing from the mountains. Your work has been an inspiration!"

In recounting the highlights of these early years of ever widening horizons there are three salient impressions which always spring to mind. They are precious memories for a man now well advanced in years. They are shared here in gratitude to my heavenly Father.

First, it was wonderful to see the way in which He moved in the lives of ministers, pastors, missionaries and other Christian leaders to let a layman like myself minister in their churches. Doors were opened wide in denominations drawn from across the whole spectrum of Christendom. With outstretched hands of welcome, I was drawn fondly into the wide circle of their fellowship.

Second, the common people of these congregations and groups took me into their hearts and into their homes with touching tenderness. Despite my rather rough and ready ways, despite my lack of polished oratory, despite the absence of esteemed professional credentials, I was shown love and loyalty that moved me mightily.

Though it was really quite late in life that at last my priorities were put in proper perspective, it was not too late for God to make up to me the "willful years." Because He is so gracious, so generous in His magnanimous manner, He enriched my days beyond my most audacious dreams as a small boy in the African bush. The good work He had begun in my life, then, He was faithful to carry on in joyous ways.

Third, it simply must be stated here that He has become to me a dear and constant Companion. It is His quiet presence, His unique Person, His enduring patience that have drawn me to Him in intense affection. Standing still, in awe, wonder and appreciation, I am humbled by the "Wonder o' the Wind" of His lovely Spirit who has moved upon my spirit and will all these years. What noble hope He gives to us who walk with *Him!*